M000103969

DO BETTER!

DO BETTER!

HOW ONE FATHER GAINED WISDOM FROM TEXTING HIS TEEN DAUGHTER

NORMAN W. HOLDEN

ISBN 978-1-7362203-0-6 (eBook)
ISBN 978-1-7362203-1-3 (Paperback Edition)
ISBN 978-1-7362203-2-0 (Hardcover Edition)

Library of Congress Cataloging-in-Publication has been applied for.

Book cover and interior design by C'EST BEAU DESIGNS

Printed and bound in the United States of America
First printing 2021

Published by NWH Holdings, LLC
Conifer, Colorado, USA

www.dobetterwisdom.com

FAM020000 FAMILY & RELATIONSHIPS / Parenting / Fatherhood

CONTENTS

DEDICATION

To my daughter, Emily, who inspired me to take this path. Thank you!
To my sons, Owen and Jackson, who unknowingly were in my thoughts
when I was sending daily messages to their sister.
Most importantly to my wife, Jean. Without her love and friendship,
I would have a whole lot less of value to share.

INTRODUCTION

To be clear, I am not a therapist, licensed professional, counselor, academic, or theologian. I am, however, like many in this great nation, an everyday man, a husband, and a father of three. Without fail, I get up each day and meet a challenging job head-on. Now a leader and business executive in the construction industry, I am a quintessential example that hard work does pay off. As someone who has worked his way up from a laborer through the ranks to senior leadership, I can honestly say I have earned my keep. I am a grateful American who has been fortunate to experience the American Dream.

I was born and raised in a rural part of Northern New Hampshire, a small town with an old name called Tamworth. A student of rural blue-collar life, my foundation was formed on solid values, good manners, and honest work. Growing up, I had my struggles—like most—yet I learned to persevere. The result transformed me into a humble patriot and an original, no-nonsense, straight-talking New Englander. I cannot think of a better way to express it other than I am damn proud of my American roots.

I am an observer of history and life's many experiences. I also enjoy seeking and trying to understand life's deeper meaning. One of the nice benefits of a career in construction is the opportunity to travel, especially if you work for a larger firm. I have had the fortune of working all around the lower forty-eight and abroad. I've been involved in ventures of varying sizes, from simple house foundations to multibillion dollar mega projects. It has exposed me to a great number of different places, people, cultures, and experiences. Adding to that, I've been fortunate to further my education by obtaining varying degrees, which also provides a wealth of insight to tap into. With over thirty years of experience managing and or leading others, you would think that I could successfully navigate one of the most important relationships in my life. Regrettably, effectively leading thousands of construction workers does not equate to success in parenting.

Written as events occurred, this account is the convergence of three personal voyages: a pilgrimage of self-introspection; a search to understand the insights of wisdom; and, most importantly, a father's journey to improve his relationship with his daughter. This is one father's attempt to bridge the gap of years of lackluster parental communication. The precursor of these events is the result of a decade of what consisted mostly of unimaginative comments and repetitive questioning regarding the status of school and general affairs. Regrettably, at the time, I felt incapable of offering exceptional guidance or parental pearls of wisdom beneficial for a young daughter's life.

This book is the culmination of a yearlong endeavor to share what is sometimes hard to say in person and, as well, correct some my personal relational shortcomings. Many of the thoughts, ideas, and pithy insights displayed within the following pages are mostly mine. With that disclaimer, I also needed some help dressing things up. Maybe a lot of help. Thankfully, there are countless quotes from more inspiring thought leaders than me. I hope my story and the personal anecdotes within resonate with you, the reader. Hopefully at a minimum, this book will help to inspire other wayward fathers in their efforts to improve communication with their daughters (and sons).

PART ONE

Looking for Solutions

THE GENESIS

PURE FRUSTRATION CREATED THE spark. I was frustrated with my adult daughter's behavior and my inability to understand her perspective or effectively communicate with her. Emily, our oldest of three, had recently graduated with her bachelor's degree in just three years, which is quite an accomplishment in our eyes. We were immensely proud parents, yet things were headed down an unexpected path.

After graduation, in lieu of moving out into the workforce and world, Emily had returned home without a whole lot of direction, and we (Emily, my wife, and I) were all stuck in this haze of disillusionment. Frustrations transitioned into heightened tempers, heated discussions, and one-way conversations, which most times produced a stone-silent daughter. I felt like I was failing as a parent. As an effective leader within my profession, able to communicate, actively listen, and clearly ascertain results, I was nowhere close to achieving the same results with my daughter. I had to find another way to bridge the gap.

I was not sure how best to connect, so I adapted. I moved to a more acceptable mode of communication: texting. While communicating to my daughter face-to-face would have been preferable, it seemed to be easier to convey my thoughts through the conduit of her default language of texting. What initially started as a two-day gesture to provide an uplifting message soon became a daily ritual. I found that trying to provide verbal guidance, advice, or feedback was reluctantly received as a "lecture from dad" and tended to be rejected on the spot. And yes, admittedly a few of my texts still come across as lectures. What is a dad supposed to do?

My new journey, which originally started as an effort to boost my daughter's self-esteem and confidence as well as counter the misguided counseling and harsh words from a few of her so-called college friends, turned into a daily labor of love. A commitment to better connect. It quickly transformed into a personal pursuit to share wisdom, knowledge, and the meaning of life—to the best of my ability. My messages consisted of all that I should have communicated many years earlier. To fully appreciate the position that I had found myself in, we must dig a little deeper.

As was mentioned in the introduction, I am a regular guy. Like many men my age (early 50s), I was raised in a loving yet very patriarchal environment, with my paternal grandparents leading the way. Both New Englanders, they lived through the Great Depression, World War II, and the subsequent postwar economic boom. My immediate family included my parents, my younger sister of six years, and me.

It is important to address my relationship with my sister, as our age difference did not induce a great deal of interaction during her transition into adolescence. During her informative years, I was gone; I had moved on to community college and life. I do not bring this up to assign blame, only to identify the missed opportunity to experience this key transition in life with her. Through introspection, I realized that there was nothing in my upbringing that truly prepared me to understand what an adolescent girl was going to experience or what support was essential.

To further compound this lack of firsthand knowledge, when my daughter reached this same transition point in her life, I took a job that inadvertently caused me to travel for work for a seven-year period. Yes, you heard it right. In October 2008, just after her eleventh birthday, I boarded a plane to work in Dubai, UAE. Regrettably, I arrived just in time to watch the global economic meltdown of the Great Recession from 7,800 miles away from home. My plans for our family to live together in another country and experience other cultures quickly evaporated. Soon, my ability to provide for my family was now tied to working away from home to the point that I felt like a visitor in my own home. I am not complaining. I was gainfully employed; we were all healthy; and we were doing relatively well under the circumstances. The obvious downside and the result of my decisions translated into me becoming an absentee father. My wife took on the burden of raising three kids while I was building projects in the Gulf Coast of Texas and Louisiana, then later in British Columbia, Canada.

Now in her early twenties, I came to realize that while my daughter had been raised in a loving home, she grew up in an era of inflated self-esteem through her upbringing, education, and interactions with social media. In a societal environment where everyone was special, it meant everyone received ribbons for participation, no one kept score, and no one lost. If you happened to be different or fell short in any way, it was not your fault; you had simply fallen victim to someone else's wrongdoing or were not as privileged as others in society. Couple this mindset with being the first generation to be raised with "in your face" technology, social media, and online videos where everyone is special and all things in life are portrayed from a favorable light, I felt unprepared and ill-equipped to compete for my daughter's attention or see the world through her eyes. It is no wonder my daughter struggled, and it is abundantly clear to me now how we reached this crossroad.

Looking back, I am sure I offered such sage advice as, "Suck it up and deal with it," or similarly anecdotal guidance. I hope I was more caring than that, yet you get the idea. Unfortunately, it is safe to say that there was probably not a lot of empathy coming from the adult in the conversation.

I can say with confidence that when Emily was preadolescent, she was very much a daddy's girl, and I was no different than many—an openly doting dad. Unfortunately, I did not prepare for what was going to naturally occur. Yes, I could have done some homework. I am sure there were plenty of reference books, medical journals, and such to rely upon. Yet why educate yourself when you can fake it until you make it? Regrettably, this was too important for a passive or thickheaded approach. Unfortunately, at the time I was too consumed by work, worried about earning a living and providing for my family, to know the difference. Did I mention that I am normal guy? Additionally, I neither understood nor appreciated the intentional grip and strength of the social media tentacles that had a firm hold on her psyche. Frankly, at the time, no one recognized the long-term impact of this new technology on our life.

What was about to occur was a pure shot in the dark. Frankly, it felt like a last-ditch effort to correct the past, mend a fractured relationship, and bring us closer than ever before. I desperately wanted for this to work.

Emily and me on the evening of her graduation from CSU
—May 18, 2019

MONTH ONE
THE START OF SOMETHING BETTER

THROUGH MY DAILY MESSAGES, it was my goal to not only share my thoughts and beliefs, but, more importantly, I had hoped this would create the conversations and communication that we both desperately needed. Through this endeavor, I strived to be the best example I could. I shared many of my own words as well as the words from some of the greatest people who have lived. Additionally, as a business executive for many years, my personal development, focus, and passion has been geared toward the skills and practice of leadership. The principles that served me well over my years in business and life are sprinkled throughout. Yes, they are not all original thoughts, yet it is how I firmly see the world. Soon, the spark of this new idea morphed into a daily ritual.

Lastly, please excuse any bad sentence structure or shorthand texting lingo. With the exception of the dates, the following excerpts are the original, unaltered text messages that I sent to my daughter. Some may question my unorthodox texting style. Yes, believe it or not, I actually typed full, unabbreviated messages without using silly cryptic emoji code. I wrote in full words and used periods, punctuation, "greetings" and "Love, Dad." Call me old school, but I believe in the formal structure of the written language—as if we lived and communicated in a pretechnological world when people spoke directly in a handwritten letter. My style will not earn me a medal in speed texting, yet it does honestly convey my sincerest desire to communicate to my daughter.

Thursday, August 29

Emily,

You are a leader of yourself! You, more than anyone else, control your destiny. Face the challenges in front of you with a positive attitude. Be happy and enjoy the gifts you have been given. Make the most of each and every day!

I love you!

Dad

Friday, August 30

Emily,

We are all presented with many personal challenges throughout our lives. How we react to said challenges is truly what defines us. It is not the poisonous words of hurtful people that define us. Having a positive moral compass, good character, strong values, and unwavering ethics are the true measurables. You have these and much more to be proud of.

Have a great day!

Love, Dad

Saturday, August 31

Good Morning, Emily!

Sorry I missed you this morning. I hope you have a great day. Stay positive and be happy with who you are. Your current situation is not permanent, and better things will come to you. Be true to yourself, and love who you are.

P.S. These have been my personal thoughts and beliefs and not something simply copied or read from a book.

Love, Dad

Sunday, September 1

Emily,

Sorry that my message is later than the past few days. Today's thoughts are simple: know that your family will always love you, and we will always be there in your corner. In the loving words of my Cousin Roxanne, "Do Better!"

Love, Dad

Monday, September 2

Labor Day

No message sent. I must have taken the day off.

Tuesday, September 3

Hey, Emily!

I hope you had a great day. Mine ended better than it started.

My message today is simple. The fears we face internally lack teeth. No different than the first time you rode a bike or drove a car—the fears that build up inside us are kitty cats dressed up in lions' clothing. There's nothing there.

It's good to see you smile! You should do it more often.

Love, Dad

Wednesday, September 4

Afternoon, Em!

Hi, from super-hot Phoenix! Holy crap! All the pithy quotes have been sweated out of me.

Do Better!

Love, Dad

Thursday, September 5

Good Morning, Emily!

Make the most of your day. Do not be satisfied with status quo. Push yourself into uncomfortable waters. That is the only way we grow as people.

Love, Dad

Friday, September 6

Morning, Em! Happy Friday!

Today's message is simple: stay true to yourself and follow your heart.

Love, Dad

Saturday, September 7

Morning Again, Emily!

Growth cannot happen without risk and failure, even when the immediate results are not the best. Without doing so we risk great results in the future. You must hold yourself accountable to the results ("the do") and not the activities ("the try") to achieve them.

"Do or do not, there is no try."

—Yoda

Love, Dad

Sunday, September 8

Good Morning, Em!

Take a moment today and pause to reflect on friends, family, your health, and the beautiful environment that we live in. We are truly blessed! Have a great day!

Love, Dad

Good Morning, Sunshine!

If you want to be more confident, behave in confident ways. You can change your behavior and allow yourself to risk failure. Don't be afraid to take on tasks that you have little knowledge of. Be transparent about your level of knowledge or experience with given tasks, but do those things that are outside your comfort zone.

Love, Dad

Morning, Em!

Focus on full-body wellness (mind, body, and soul). It's vital that you find and maintain a healthy balance of continuous education, exercise, diet, sleep, inner faith (or spirituality), and fulfilling relationships. Form these habits earlier in your life as they will help you find happiness and will pay dividends down the road.

Love, Dad

Good Morning, Emily!

Servant leadership is a very powerful skill to be learned and practiced. Helping, serving, and seeing to the needs of others before your own needs will earn you eminence as you radiate joy. Offering this service should be done without an expectation of recognition, reciprocation, or self-promotion.

Love, Dad

Morning, Em!

When people use responses such as "I'll try!" or "I was going to!" or "I was planning to!" they are by default spreading false intentions. The recipient of these messages receives a trust tax in lieu of reassurance that meaningful action will occur.

Have a great day!

Love, Dad

Friday, September 13

Afternoon, Em!

The day almost flew by me, yet my thoughts are not constrained by time. There is truth to the power of a positive attitude. It will get you through difficult obstacles. Stay positive and good things will happen.

Love, Dad

Saturday, September 14

Good Morning, Emily!

Have confidence in the knowledge that your family believes in you. We love you, and your future is unlimited.

Have a great day!

Love, Dad

Sunday, September 15

Morning, Em!

I hope you start to feel better. Take care of yourself. Get out and get some fresh air; it will help your recovery. Be positive and be better!

Love, Dad

Good Morning, Emily!

Time: It is a unique resource that is totally irreplaceable, and there is no substitute for it. We all receive the same 1,440 minutes per day. We cannot buy, rent, or save it for future use. Yesterday's time is gone forever, and we can never get it back. Everything we do requires it. Do not waste it on idle activities of no worth. Make the most of the time you have be given; it is truly precious.

Love, Dad

Good Morning, Emily!

Be okay with being okay. Be good with the struggles that life presents us. Never lose face or family as a result of the challenges in life. We all feel them. Perseverance (grit) is doing something well despite the difficulty we typically deal with while achieving success. Always be steadfast, be strong, and be better.

Love, Dad

Wednesday, September 18

Good Morning, Sunshine!

While continuous improvement is a noble effort, chasing perfection is a fool's errand. Push yourself to improve and become more skilled where your passions take you.

I hope you have a great day!

Love, Dad

Thursday, September 19

Good Afternoon, Em!

The power of internal affirmation is your ability to quiet the internal voice that can help you to challenge and overcome self-sabotaging and negative thoughts.

Love, Dad

Friday, September 20

Good Morning, Emily!

We grow according to the demands that we make on ourselves. Our growth is based upon what we consider to be achievable and attainable. If we demand little of ourselves, we will remain stunted or stagnant. Expect and demand more from yourself. By failing to do so, you are only letting yourself down.

Love, Dad

Saturday, September 21

Good Morning Again, Em!

While popular culture (and many in the media) may have us think differently, popularity, self-promotion, and/or extroverted outer beauty are not virtues. The personal values of Integrity, Accountability, Dependability, Dignity, Honor, Responsibility, Intelligence, Common Sense, Service, Humility, and Grit are true measures of one's worth. The consistent adherence and practice of these values (and many more) will boost your inner self-confidence 1,000x over shallow efforts to impress others.

Love, Dad

Sunday, September 22

Good Morning, Emily!

"Beauty is in the eye of the beholder" was first attributed to the author Margaret Wolfe Hungerford. I believe the "eye of the beholder" can both be inner- and exterior-facing. While we will be naturally drawn to others for many reasons, one's inner beauty (heart, mind, and soul) and how we outwardly display this love is more awe-inspiring.

Please know that you will always be beautiful to your mother and me.

Love, Dad

Happy First Day of Autumn!

The Navy Seals have a saying: "The only easy day was yesterday." While the majority of normal people are not elite soldiers, all of us face difficult challenges going through life. Frankly, if you come out on the other end without a few battle scars, then you really haven't lived a good life. Those battle scars are the result of failures, struggles, missteps, poor decisions, or events where others have hurt you. In total, they are all powerful life lessons to be embraced, reflected upon, and used as motivation to continually improve.

Yes, life is hard at times, yet we all need to make most of the time we have been blessed with.

Love, Dad

Good Morning, Em!

Initiative is defined as "the ability to assess and initiate things independently" or "the power or opportunity to act or take charge before others do." Taking the initiative signals to others that you are not going to be passive about your beliefs. It also illustrates passion and the value of grit. Normally, people on the receiving end of your initiative are very grateful.

For example: your initiative this past Friday to invite your mother and me out for a walk and dinner was greatly appreciated.

Have a great day!

Love, Dad

Good Afternoon, Emily!

Second behind the extension of love to others, trust is a key part of servant leadership. One of President Reagan's famous dictums was, "Trust, but verify." Therefore, extending smart trust is one of the best things you can do for the recipient and for yourself. Being overly trusting or, on the opposite end of the spectrum, not extending trust at all, will be at great personal expense to yourself.

Trust should never be taken for granted.

Love, Dad

Good Morning, Em!

4 Don'ts & 1 Do!

Don't be taken for granted.

Don't allow others to walk on you.

Don't ever let a man tell you can't do something because you're a woman.

Don't let others govern your life.

BUT ...

Do trust yourself and have confidence in who you are!

Love, Dad

Good Morning Again, Em!

I've never understood why some people choose not to leave their hometown. I realize for some it may be a matter of financial means or a fear of the unknown; however, others decidedly prefer to remain close to home for their entire life. These people may be more family centric than me, yet I believe there is lost opportunity in not going out into the world. Great joy comes from the experiences of seeing new places, cultures, and people. I hope you choose to explore.

Love, Dad

Saturday, September 28

Good Morning, Emily!

Today's message is short and sweet. Be true to yourself.
Be authentic and be real.

Love, Dad

Sunday, September 29

Good Morning, Emily!

Sometimes it's important to stop and reflect upon the
gifts we have been blessed with. Life and all of its
wonders are amazingly beautiful. Along the journey,
make it a frequent habit to stop and smell the flowers,
enjoy the vistas of life, and embrace those whom
you love.

Have a great day!

Love, Dad

Monday, September 30

Good Morning, Emily!

Accountability creates independence and trust; whereas the culture of victimization (portraying yourself as the victim) creates dependency and distrust. Unfortunately, we have become a victimization society where no one takes personal responsibility and accountability for their actions. This is a chronic problem for many; however, it can be easily avoided by becoming a strong leader who holds herself accountable.

Love, Dad

MONTH TWO
MESSAGES FROM AFAR

In early October 2020, my wife, Jean, and I were visiting Ireland for the first time. At this point in my texting journey, I had not shared with Jean what I was up to. It was still a test of the "Father's Broadcasting System," and maybe only a test. Frankly, I had not truly conveyed to my daughter why I decided to connect through daily messaging.

My overall agenda was not fully baked, but it was simple. As time passed, it was my goal for the messages to offer some hope or direction, and I anticipated that life would improve for everyone involved. Simple, right? Only a desperate father would expect breakthrough (or pain-free) results from such a straightforward approach. Did I mention that I am not a therapist?

However, now in the middle of an incredible vacation, I had to explain why I had this urgent need to take a text break each morning while traveling the Irish countryside. After a brief explanation, Jean was on board and even offered some of her own insights. Thankfully, my wife is a patient person. I had a good excuse, and it was not related to work back home. It also did not hurt that we were having a great time in a beautiful country.

Tuesday, October 1

Good Morning, Em!

You can do or be anything you want in life. Your level of success simply comes down to your level of effort, invested time, hard work, practice, and determination toward your chosen endeavor. There is no guarantee that you will achieve your vision of your ultimate success, yet don't let anyone tell you that you can't do it.

Love, Dad

Wednesday, October 2

Good Morning, Emily!

Setting goals and breaking down the required steps is a crucial first part of achieving a life dream or accomplishment. Identify your destination and plan the pathway. All great accomplishments always start with one first step. Don't be afraid to take the first step.

Love, Dad

Thursday, October 3

Good Morning, Emily!

No matter your goal or destination, remember to always keep the faith of higher beliefs, values, and character.

Have a great day!

Love, Dad

Friday, October 4

Happy Birthday, Emily!

Your mother and I are wishing you a day filled with happiness and a year filled with joy. One of our happiest moments was the day you came into our life.

Have a great day!

Love, Dad

Saturday, October 5

Good Morning, Em!

Understand your strengths and know what you're good at. Being self-aware will bring you confidence, which builds success. These two actions combined are a multiplying force.

Love, Dad

Sunday, October 6

Good Afternoon, Emily!

Faith. Faith is our confidence or trust in a person, thing, or concept. It is something that you can easily lose, yet it is not something you can buy more of. When faith is lost, it is simply set aside until trust has been restored. The more trust you have will indeed expand your faith.

Love, Dad

Monday, October 7

Good Morning, Em!

Inner self-discipline: Many view the word "discipline" as being negative, when without it our dreams, ideas, and inspirations would never come to reality. Having strong inner self-discipline is the bridge required to achieve our goals.

Love, Dad

Tuesday, October 8

Good Morning, Em!

Do what's right even when no one is looking. This is a true measure of character, and it may even require you to do something that is unpopular.

Love, Dad

Wednesday, October 9

Good Morning, Emily!

I remember when you were younger, your mother and I shared with you and your brothers the difference between a "want" and a "need." As you get older, the cost of choosing poorly can be more financially detrimental. It's important to live within your means. All too often I meet people who are struggling, working from paycheck to paycheck, living beyond their means and without a financial plan.

Love, Dad

Thursday, October 10

Good Morning, Emily!

Your word is your bond. It is the quickest and easiest way to establish (and break) trust. Early on in my career, I learned a "Bakerism" by Daniel L Baker: "Your tongue and your toes should always be aligned." You're only as good as your word, and your actions need to match.

Have a great day!

Love, Dad

Friday, October 11

Good Morning, Emily!

It's okay not to know the answer to the life question: "What do I want to be when I grow up?" Even in my early 50s, I struggle with it from time to time. Some people instinctively know the answer, while I would hazard to guess the majority of us are uncertain. I think the important thing is to find work that you enjoy doing that offers you a sense of accomplishment, fulfillment, and purpose. Do this work with a sense of pride and have fun. In the course of doing so, lead with your heart, then love and serve others. By doing these things, you'll have the answer many times throughout your life.

Love, Dad

Saturday, October 12

Good Morning, Emily!

Karma: I'm a firm believer that you reap what you sow. Simply, you get back what you put out into the world.

Love, Dad

Sunday, October 13

Good Morning, Em!

The Golden Rule: Treat people the way you want to be treated. This is the easiest rule to follow and should be judiciously applied to all we do.

Love, Dad

Monday, October 14

Good Morning, Emily!

Sense of pride: Pride is considered one of the Seven Deadly Sins; therefore, if pride = hubris (or vanity), then I would agree. However, if being modestly proud of yourself, your friends, your family, your home, your company, or your country is a sin, then I strongly disagree.

I'm proud of you!

Love, Dad

Tuesday, October 15

Good Morning, Em!

Decision making and intuition (leading with your gut): I was once told (and am a firm believer) that a women's sense of intuition is better than a man's. Using your intuition is not as simple as it seems, and a decision is not always a clear black-or-white judgement. With practice, you can learn to better assess your intuitive experiences, which can aid in making better decisions.

Love, Dad

Wednesday, October 16

Good Morning, Emily!

Love your family and friends like there is no tomorrow. None of us have a guaranteed duration in life; therefore, we must not squander what opportunities we have been given.

Love, Dad

Thursday, October 17

Good Morning, Em!

Best of luck today! Hold your head high; be confident and open-minded. There is a power to positive thinking, so approach each exchange with a positive attitude and your star will shine brilliantly. Remember these earlier jobs in life are just stepping-stones that lead to greater opportunities.

Love, Dad

Friday, October 18

Good Morning, Emily!

Patience is a virtue. This is a character trait that many of us struggle with, especially in our youth. I know I did and still do at times. What has helped me is the realization that there are some things in this world that you can control, yet the majority of other things you cannot. Recognizing the latter when they occur and taking a deep breath before reacting will reduce your level of frustration and will help you to temper your response.

Love, Dad

Saturday, October 19

Good Evening, Em!

All of us want to feel a sense of belonging and connection with others. This fulfillment can only truly be obtained through personal relationships, not virtually. The facade of likes, views, and posts will never replace a natural human bond or relationship. Even this text, while well intended, is a sparse substitute for face-to-face conversation.

Love, Dad

Sunday, October 20

Good Morning, Emily!

Hard work and the desire to persevere = grit. It's good to be gritty!

Love, Dad

Monday, October 21

Good Morning, Sunshine!

Don't allow yourself to get down when things don't seem to work out the way you want or hoped. Just when you think a door has closed, another will always open.

Have a great day!

Love, Dad

Tuesday, October 22

Good Morning, Em!

Change. Some will say that we humans don't like change, and we struggle to adapt to it. When, in fact, we are naturally wired to identify changes in our environment. This is the skill that kept us from being eaten when we first arrived on the scene. Our original survival depended upon our ability to recognize and adapt to change. Fast-forward to this day and age, and our resistance to change is most likely tied to our habits. If you find yourself struggling with change, look for the habits that are holding you back, then positively address them. Adapting to change and being nimble will keep you ahead of the pack.

Love, Dad

Wednesday, October 23

Good Morning, Em!

Make smart choices. Understand and think through the many possible outcomes from your decision(s). Think about how your decision affects others first, and then worry about yourself. Making mistakes and dumb choices is expected because we are not perfect; however, we have the ability to assess the risks and rewards before making a decision. The key is to do so before, rather than after. If things go awry, don't blame others; take responsibility for your decisions and actions.

Love, Dad

Good Morning, Emily!

Don't be afraid to take the road less traveled; the journey may take you to places that you wouldn't have imagined.

Best of luck on your interview today. I know you will do well. "Break a leg!"

Love, Dad

Good Morning, Emily!

"The pursuit of perfection is a fool's errand!"

—Unknown

I'm not sure who first coined this phrase, yet I recently heard it stated and couldn't agree more. However, I would temper that statement by expressing my strong belief in continuous improvement. We always have room to become better.

"Do Better!"

—Roxanne Smith

Love, Dad

Saturday, October 26

Good Morning, Sunshine!

Hate is a strong feeling and attitude. It's okay to say you're unhappy or you dislike something, yet to truly hate something or someone is extremely negative and should be used sparingly.

Love, Dad

Sunday, October 27

Good Morning, Emily!

The benefit of sharing wisdom is lessened if it is not requested and/or appreciated by the recipient.

Should I continue?

Love, Dad

Good Morning, Em!

It is said that the American Dream is dead. By definition, it is "the ideal by which equality of opportunity is available to any American, allowing the highest aspirations and goals to be achieved," and it "is achieved through sacrifice, risk-taking, and hard work, rather than by chance." I believe the American Dream is alive and well. You will have to work extremely hard to create opportunities for others and yourself to achieve the desired outcome, yet it does exist. Live your dream!

Love, Dad

Good Morning, Sunshine!

Scarcity vs. Abundance Mentality: Scarcity mentality is nothing more than self-preservation. ("I have to undermine or climb over you to achieve my goals.") Whereas abundance mentality is the ideal that if you work to lift up others around you, there will be growth opportunities for everyone. Avoid the scarcity cave!

Love, Dad

Wednesday, October 30

Good Morning, Em!

The hardest part of anything worth doing is getting started, yet the initial friction (and sometimes failure) is a necessary part of the equation and is worth the struggle.

Love, Dad

Thursday, October 31

Good Morning, Em!

Happy Halloween! It is the darkest just before there is light. Similarly, it is the coldest just before dawn. Both symbiotic reactions tell us that when we think things are at their worst, our situation will soon change for the better. Do Better!

Love, Dad

P.S. Have fun and please be safe tonight!

MONTH THREE
GIVING THANKS

By month three, I have firmly settled into my daily routine of writing, researching, and sharing pieces of wisdom and general insight, with a few life and history lessons scattered about. At this point, I am unsure if my messages are having their desired effect. It has been two months of daily communication, and there has been zero reply in response. I have still not conveyed out loud or by text the reason behind my resent messaging. I am not sure why I expected Emily to reciprocate my unsolicited messages, yet I did. Unfortunately, the Internet Age has conditioned us to expect a response. Frankly, she did not owe me one.

In late October, I finally broke and asked (via text), "Should I continue?" Her response lifted my spirits: "I like getting the messages every day. It's nice to wake up to/rely on." Thankful for her answer, I had my affirmation, a positive confirmation that my efforts were not in vain. The next step was going to be a whole lot tougher. It became clear that I could no longer hide behind my daily texts; I had to have an adult conversation to share the why behind my motives. A home cooked dinner and a face-to-face conversation were on the menu.

In early November, upon returning home from a business trip, I invited Emily to join me for dinner. After a good meal, a little red wine, and a heart-to-heart talk, it became clear that our relationship and its foundations had been reinforced by my efforts. It also became apparent that I needed to continue. Not just for Emily, but for both of us. This newly formed habit had unexpectantly stirred something inside of me. My spirit was awakened.

Friday, November 1

Good Morning, Emily!

Theodore Roosevelt's April 1910 Paris speech, "Citizenship in a Republic," has a very notable passage that stands the test of time. In part, "the man who is actually in the arena" requires courage, skill, and/or grit. Live life in the arena and not as a spectator.

Love, Dad

Saturday, November 2

Good Morning, Em!

To take a stand for something means you accept ownership and responsibility for the matter. It doesn't mean you are to blame, nor have you forfeited the ability to cast blame on others or your circumstances. It also doesn't mean you're right; it just means you now own it. However, you can still hold others responsible as well.

Love, Dad

Sunday, November 3

Good Morning, Sunshine!

Happiness and everything you need in life is right in front of you and surrounds you. Know you are loved.

Love, Dad

Monday, November 4

Good Morning, Emily!

You are an intelligent woman who is beautiful on the inside and out. You can do anything you put your mind to. Have a great day!

Love, Dad

P.S. Sorry I missed you last night. I'll see you later this week.

Tuesday, November 5

Good Morning, Emily!

It's Election Day!

Our extraordinary country is a Constitutional Republic, and one of the greatest rights (15th Amendment) we have as citizens is the right to vote for our leaders. In my opinion, when someone fails to exercise their right to vote, they have essentially forfeited their right to complain about the state of political affairs in our country. Please take this responsibility very seriously.

Love, Dad

Wednesday, November 6

Good Morning, Em!

Be committed to something bigger than yourself.

Love, Dad

Thursday, November 7

Good Morning, Emily!

Be forward looking. If you're looking behind you, you're simply reacting. Be proactive and look forward.

Love, Dad

Friday, November 8

Good Morning, Sunshine!

Life's happiness is not tied to the trappings of fame and fortune; rather, it stems from the love we give to and receive from others.

Love, Dad

Saturday, November 9

Good Morning, Em!

The investment of time and energy is required to achieve any goal.

Love, Dad

Sunday, November 10

Good Morning, Emily!

Live a meaningful life—one full of love, purpose, and joy.

Love, Dad

Monday, November 11

Good Morning, Sunshine!

Today is a day of Remembrance! In 1918, at the 11th hour of the 11th day of the 11th month, the hostilities of World War I finally came to an end. Later, in 1938, November 11 was formally set aside in the US as Armistice Day, which we now know as Veterans Day. While today is the official remembrance holiday, I believe that we should honor all that have served every day, as it takes a special kind of courage to serve a cause greater than one's self with the knowledge that you may be called upon to make the ultimate sacrifice for the freedom of others.

Happy Veterans Day!

Love, Dad

Tuesday, November 12

Good Morning, Emily!

A self-reflection from your old father: "Over time, we begin to forget what we have learned along the journey to know what we have mastered." This recently came to me in a leadership course that I was attending. I firmly believe that the mastery of any subject or skill is a limitless journey (a mountain without a top).

Love, Dad

Wednesday, November 13

Good Morning, Em!

In the realm of possibility, possibilities are unlimited, and there are no wrong answers.

Love, Dad

Thursday, November 14

Good Morning, Emily!

To answer the questions you are dwelling in, you must first get unstuck from the answers you may have.

Love, Dad

Friday, November 15

Good Morning, Emily!

Be as kind to yourself as you are to others. Most times we are our own worst critic; we tend to be harder on ourself than we need to be.

Love, Dad

Saturday, November 16

Good Morning, Em!

It is important to reflect upon the context of our life that forms, colors, and shades our beliefs, decisions, and actions. True and honest self-reflection will lead you to strengthen your emotional intelligence, which in most cases is more important than one's IQ.

Love, Dad

Sunday, November 17

Good Morning, Emily!

Do not let the opinion of others concern you. The only opinion of yourself that matters is your own. However, honest, constructive, and positive feedback from those who know us best is invaluable.

Love, Dad

Good Morning, Em!

Always remember: we before me!

Love, Dad

Good Morning, Sunshine!

Practice what you preach! This original maxim points to the hypocrite who fails to follow his or her own advice. In sharing my thoughts and beliefs with you over the past few months, I have found myself reflecting upon the authenticity of my words and being. I must ask myself, *Am I being true to my words?* If we falter or fall short (which will occur), we must be timely to restore integrity to honor our words.

Love, Dad

Good Morning, Em!

Time: Why is a simple universal measurement standard so important to us? Why is it that when we are young, time is so expansive, yet when we get older it seems to speed up exponentially? The incremental value of a second, an hour, or a day did not change, yet this fleeting resource appears to speed up. Similar to grains of sand pouring through an hourglass, maybe it is the fear that we have less of it left, or maybe the value we place on it becomes more real. I'm going to believe in the latter explanation, and I hope you do as well.

Love, Dad

Good Morning, Sunshine!

You may be able to fool others, yet you will never be able to fool yourself. Be genuine inside and out.

Love, Dad

Friday, November 22

Good Morning, Em!

Remove the cancers from your life: complacency, misplaced ego, laziness, envy, jealousy, hatred, and lust for fame; instead, fill the void with love.

Love, Dad

Saturday, November 23

Good Morning, Emily!

In life's endeavors, focus your time and energy on the journey and not the destination.

Love, Dad

Sunday, November 24

Good Morning, Em!

The harder you work (and love) the more you will live.

Love, Dad

Monday, November 25

Good Morning, Sunshine!

The meaning of life: While I am certainly not a scientist or theologian, I have lived a full life thus far. One containing life's expected (and unexpected) twists and turns, ups and downs, similar to those roller coasters that you want to avoid. A normal life for most. In my half-plus century of being, I'm not sure if I yet grasp the true meaning of life; however, I can say with some confidence that I understand what it means to live a meaningful life.

Love, Dad

Tuesday, November 26

Good Morning, Em!

Confident, resourceful, creative, capable, and resilient people do not emote an outward display of their emotions or feelings at the level that our society has become accustomed to witnessing. Instead, they limit their personal sharing through thoughtful conversations with close friends, confidants, or family.

Love, Dad

Good Morning, Emily!

Leaders ... Born vs. Made: As someone who has studied and practiced leadership principles and is passionate about the effective act of leadership, I would like to share my beliefs on this often debated conundrum.

No different than a successful athlete, musician, artist, medical professional, or master carpenter, one must develop the skills necessary to achieve a high level of success. With that being said, one must also be endowed with certain natural abilities (aptitude or gifts) required to transform a practiced skill into mastery. As an example, just because a person has a passion for and practices playing the violin does not mean they have the ability to become a peak performing musician or a first violinist in a major orchestra.

Likewise, some of us become authentic leaders through the natural development of our given skills and the effective practice of servant leadership through the act of being a leader. Others, while exposed to the tenets of leadership, will never progress to the point where they have earned the trust of those individuals that they wish to lead.

In short, the answer to this question must be both; leaders are born and only through mastery made great.

Love, Dad

Thursday, November 28

Good Morning, Emily! Happy Thanksgiving!

Thanksgiving was intended to be a day of reflection, a day to pause and be thankful for the blessings in our life and not a perversion of self-indulgence, sales, and commercialization. Unfortunately, the original context of this holiday has been lost. Unlike the early pilgrims and the indigenous peoples that first inhabited this land, most in our society today have not suffered nor can they appreciate what it is like to struggle for one's survival. We would be wise to reflect upon our heritage and cherish these moments.

Love, Dad

Friday, November 29

Good Morning, Em!

Please spread the word: the world does not need any more high-maintenance people!

Love, Dad

Saturday, November 30

Good Morning, Sunshine!

When in doubt, work it out before making any rash decisions.

Love, Dad

MONTH FOUR
A MONTH OF INTROSPECTION

In early December 2019, I completed a two-week leadership development course[1] in New York that had a profound effect on me and my way of being. My eyes were opened to early childhood experiences (specifically two crucible events) that unknowingly altered my future. My inability to physically perform on the playing field and the distractions keeping me from being able to excel in the classroom were the two primary culprits.

Eventually I found a medium that I could excel in that became "work." My payoff for the racket called work is as follows: I was able to excel and dominate, which allowed me to win. Unfortunately, in doing so I allowed this to become a "work only" life sentence that caused me to ignore the important things in life (family, personal relationships, hobbies, true fulfillment, and my well-being). Do not get me wrong, I also benefited from this motivating force in my life. My desire to outwork others around me has propelled me forward and created much opportunity. However, it did come at a cost.

---

1 JMW's "Being a Leader and the Effective Exercise of Leadership" (JMW, 2019).

You may wonder why this discovery is relevant to my relationship with my daughter. I realized that having this knowledge and being able to understand one's personal early developmental events and their corresponding effects is a powerful tool. Frankly, I wish I had discovered this thirty years ago. I believe that personal self-awareness (EQ) is more potent than IQ, yet when properly dispensed, together they are invaluable. Ultimately, this experience helped to open my eyes to my old way of being and propelled me toward a desire to change. It motivated me to continue my chosen journey to Do Better!

Sunday, December 1

Good Morning, Emily!

I often tell young people entering into Baker for the first time that we will intentionally put them in where the water is in over their heads. We do this primarily to see how they will instinctively react. Will they raise their hand and ask for help, or will they instead pretend that everything is fine until they drown themselves? Or, worse, will they take others down with them? There is no shame in asking for help or saying you don't know how to do something, so long as the request and your effort to learn are genuine. The truth is, we will never know our true potential until we swim into the deep water.

Love, Dad

Monday, December 2

Good Morning, Em!

Smiles and laughter are contagious; be selfless and pass them along.

Love, Dad

Tuesday, December 3

Good Morning, Emily!

People who play it safe their entire life will never reach their full potential.

Love, Dad

P.S. Another thought for you this morning: What is the future you wish to create for yourself? Start there and work back to the present.

Wednesday, December 4

Good Morning, Sunshine!

Our mindset and attitude determine how we show up.

Love, Dad

Good Morning, Em!

The sole interest of any business should be to bring value to its internal customers (its employees) and external customers (in that order). By doing so, profits and shareholder value will ultimately be satisfied. The people that the business serves should be the ultimate focus and goal.

Love, Dad

Friday, December 6

Good Morning, Emily!

Thinking or playing small out of fear will limit your personal vision and growth.

Love, Dad

Good Morning, Em!

"A date which will live in infamy" was declared by President Franklin D. Roosevelt the day following Japan's attack on Pearl Harbor and their declaration of war on our country. An event that changed the course of history. In no way am I intending to lessen the significance of this date, yet if we truly reflect, every event of every day alters the course of the future. And that is where we should live—in the future and not in the past. It is okay to look to the past to connect the dots from life's lessons; however, to affect change we must live in the present and in a better vision of the future. This is the only way to effectively change history, not by altering, erasing, tearing down, or being stuck in what we do not agree with.

Love, Dad

Good Morning, Sunshine!

We all want to feel like our life and work have meaning, that there is a purpose behind our existence. By serving others first, you will discover the purpose and significance to this meaning.

Love, Dad

Good Morning, Emily!

Which would you prefer: a victim mindset of reacting, scarcity, and fear or an owner's mindset of abundance, love, creativity, and purpose? To me, there is only one way of being.

Love, Dad

Good Morning, Emily!

Be okay with being uncomfortable. Have a great day!

Love, Dad

Wednesday, December 11

Good Morning, Em!

Politically correct speech: The First Amendment provides us with the freedom of speech; however, it doesn't protect us from being offended by someone else's words. In society today, some feel they cannot say what they truly think for fear of possible reproach by others or negative repercussions by those that may be offended. Don't get me wrong, there is no benefit from hurtful words, yet just because you may disagree with my position on a topic doesn't automatically make what I say hate speech. Politically correct speech only dumbs down the conversation in an effort to protect those of us who have thin skin or a weak mind.

Love, Dad

Thursday, December 12

Good Morning, Sunshine!

There are only two ways of being; you're either being present in the moment or you're choosing not to. The latter is not worth the wasted energy.

Love, Dad

Good Morning, Em!

A superstition is defined as "a widely held but unjustified belief in supernatural causation, leading to certain consequences of an action or event, or a practice based on such a belief." The funny thing is, for something so unjustifiable, we all certainly seem to believe in superstitions. What are some of yours?

Have a great day!

Love, Dad

Good Morning, Emily!

Serving others is a form of personal healing.

Love, Dad

Good Morning, Sunshine!

I recently read the following verse from Luke 4:24: "Truly I tell you; no prophet is accepted in his hometown." While I know that I cannot stand in the shoes of a prophet, I hope that you will accept my ramblings for what they are.

Love, Dad

Monday, December 16

Good Morning, Emily!

Unfortunately, in society we place a high level of value on entertainers, actors, and sports figures even when their behavior is reprehensible. Last time I checked, they put their pants on one leg at a time no different than anyone else. There are more deserving people who make a greater impact and sacrifice without any fanfare. These individuals are the real leaders in our life who truly deserve the spotlight.

Love, Dad

Tuesday, December 17

Good Morning, Em!

According to Alexander Graham Bell, "When one door closes, another opens; but we often look so long and so regretfully upon the closed door that we do not see the one which has opened for us." Opportunities will only become visible if you walk through the open door.

Love, Dad

Good Morning, Emily!

Remember to honor your roots. All experiences in life (even bad ones) are foundational and make us stronger. We tend to learn more from our mistakes than our successes. Therefore, a bad experience is sometimes more valuable than a good one because it helps to positively shape us for the future.

Love, Dad

Good Morning, Sunshine!

"Ah-ha" moments are exciting, inspirational, and serve as creative opportunities for growth. Go seek them out!

Love, Dad

Good Morning, Emily!

"It always seems impossible until it's done."

—Nelson Mandela.

"Done" can be the completion of a physical task, or it could be bringing closure to those issues in our mind or past that seem to haunt us. While the physical tasks are easier to grasp, the conclusion of those mental "life sentences" are much more fulfilling.

Love, Dad

Saturday, December 21

Good Morning, Em!

"There is no hard to a whale!"

—Jerry Straus

The whale swimming through the depths of the ocean does not consider or express *hard*. Only as humans and through our language do we create hard.

Love, Dad

Sunday, December 22

Good Morning, Emily!

"This is the beginning of a new day. God has given me this day to use as I will. I can waste it or use it for good. What I do today is very important because I am exchanging a day of my life for it. When tomorrow comes, this day will be gone forever, leaving something in its place I have traded for it. I want it to be a gain, not a loss—good, not evil. Success, not failure, in order that I shall not regret the price I paid for it."

—Heartsill Wilson

Love, Dad

Monday, December 23

Good Morning, Em!

Be disciplined in your thoughts and actions. Don't feel like you must please others all the time. It's okay to say no.

Love, Dad

Tuesday, December 24

Good Morning, Sunshine!

All humans yearn to hear these words: "You are loved. You are special. You are invaluable. You will achieve great things in your life." Please be fulfilled in knowing that while I do not say them enough, they are always in my heart when I think of and see you.

Love, Dad

Wednesday, December 25

Good Morning, Emily! Merry Christmas!

While the meaning of Christmas is about much more than exchanging gifts, I was recently reminded by a peer (and friend) that the most important gift given and/or received costs nothing. The best gift that we can exchange comes from the heart. It can be the offer of support or encouragement. It can come in the form of appreciation or recognition. It can be a shared conversation, laughter, or smile. It can be the extension of help, a hug, or love. The best gifts in life have no monetary value. Celebrate the joy of Christmas in its truest form.

Love, Dad

Thursday, December 26

Good Morning, Em!

If you ever find yourself trying to answer the question, "Am I good enough?" just know that you are always good enough, and don't waste time searching for the answer.

Love, Dad

Friday, December 27

Good Morning, Em!

"Work will fill any space you give it. Claim your space."

—Dwight Mahabir.

Lead a balanced life in your work, relationships, faith, community, and health.

Love, Dad

Saturday, December 28

Good Morning, Sunshine!

Holding ourself and others accountable is the choice of love over fear.

Love, Dad

Sunday, December 29

Good Morning, Emily!

You are not your past or what people say you are. You are your vision of your future, and nothing can keep you from your destiny.

Love, Dad

Good Morning, Em!

What is the future you wish to create for yourself? Start there and work back to the present.

Love, Dad

Good Morning, Emily!

Life's Crutches: While it is comforting to know they're there when we need the support and something to lean on, the sooner we can build inner personal strength to shed the crutches in life, the better off and stronger we are going to be.

Love, Dad

MONTH FIVE
A NEW YEAR

MORE THAN A THIRD of the way through this journey of sharing, I began to reflect upon where this path would ultimately lead. Everyone's attitudes were improving, and my passion for this endeavor was building exponentially. My personal discovery was on the rise. The New Year brought a fresh perspective and a renewed interest to provide sound and sage advice.

My 2020 resolution was plainly in sight as a renewed vigor propelled me forward. With a clear goal, I knew I had to commit to this journey for eight more months. I wanted to see if a year of continuous messages would deliver better results. With my curiosity and creativity on high, I doubled down on my efforts. It took little time before I had fully immersed myself in additional reading, research, and topical learning. I sought to convey life's wisdom as I saw it. I genuinely wanted my maxims to be more than just "Dad's commentary on life."

Thankfully, my resolution to provide insightful affirmations had greater momentum. Unfortunately, my sugary treats abstinence plan failed in three weeks in a ball of flaming cookie dough. Did I mention that my wife loves to bake? Especially around the holidays, and she is particularly good at it. My sweet tooth won the battle of wills.

Good Morning, Em! Happy New Year!

The New Year is a time for personal introspection, reflection, and enacting positive change in one's life. Look for those things that you know you can Do Better! and reshape your life.

Have a great day!

Love, Dad

Good Morning, Em!

You have to be at peace with the past. Embrace it in order to be free from it, then you can live in your desired future. If you resist the past, it will only persist and be more of the same.

Love, Dad

Friday January 3

Good Morning, Sunshine!

"Inspiration is a guest that does not willingly visit the lazy."

—Pyotr Llyich Tchaikovsky

Love, Dad

Saturday, January 4

Good Morning, Em!

Being stuck along with spontaneous imagination and creativity will lead to invention.

Love, Dad

Sunday, January 5

Good Morning, Emily!

Forgiveness is a very powerful tonic for both the dispenser and the recipient of the act.

Love, Dad

Monday, January 6

Good Morning, Em!

"We often take for granted the very things that most deserve our gratitude."

—Cynthia Ozick

Love, Dad

P.S. Good luck on the start of your internship today. Ask many questions and learn as much as you can.

Tuesday, January 7

Good Morning, Sunshine!

Be grateful; be very grateful for what you have been blessed with.

Love, Dad

Wednesday, January 8

Good Morning, Em!

Be a good caretaker of things you have worked hard for. Unfortunately, today's society has become very "disposable" or wasteful. We seem to care little for the worth of many things. Unlike the past, people care less about maintaining or repairing those things that they have accumulated. Take care of your belongings and, if possible, fix them before throwing them out. And before throwing anything away, consider if it can be of value to someone else.

Love, Dad

Thursday, January 9

Good Morning, Emily

"When you are finished changing, you're finished."

—Benjamin Franklin.

The same goes for learning and continuously improving.

Love, Dad

Friday, January 10

Good Morning, Em!

"To master something is to be used by what you are mastering."

—David Spiwack

Love, Dad

Saturday, January 11

Good Morning, Emily!

More important than celebrating your own birthday is remembering to call your mom on hers. Today is Grammy Jill's birthday. That reminds me, I need to call her!

Love, Dad

Sunday, January 12

Good Morning, Em!

I believe the best meal of the day has to be breakfast, not because it is the most important, but because it is typically the first meal of a brand-new day. Being blessed with a new day is worth celebrating in style.

Love, Dad

Monday, January 13

Good Morning, Sunshine!

Through most of life we are the student, and at times
the teacher as well. It's important to have positive
and unbiased influences (good teachers, coaches, and
mentors) in our life.

Love, Dad

Tuesday, January 14

Good Morning, Em!

I heard the following quote by an unknown author
over twenty years ago that has stuck with me: "Man
does not wake up until he dies." My early and most
common interpretation was that we do not realize the
significance of something until it is too late. Recently,
I realized that one cannot truly live until we come to
grips with the fact that we will all die eventually. The
sooner we accept this, the more at ease we become and
the sooner we can get on with living.

Love, Dad

Wednesday, January 15

Good Morning, Em!

Sometimes it's best to leave things unsaid. Especially if your comments are going to intentionally hurt the recipient. I'm not saying that you shouldn't truthfully speak your mind, yet understand that once said, some things can't easily be undone. Know that sourly grumbling or saying ungrateful things can easily pierce the strongest person's heart.

Love, Dad

Thursday, January 16

Good Morning, Emily!

The saying "a rising tide lifts all boats" is commonly attributed to President John F. Kennedy. While this general truth was referring to economic policy, this concept applies to many positive circumstances. Good situations in our life will lift us internally, which will provide us with the opportunity to lift others up around us. Be a rising tide and a positive force.

Love, Dad

Friday, January 17

Good Morning, Em!

The future is never certain because it always exists as a possibility. The majority of the time, we must create opportunities and possibilities for ourselves so that our vision of the future will develop as we envision it to be.

Love, Dad

Saturday, January 18

Good Morning, Sunshine!

Don't let others limit your dreams and aspirations. Be the master of your destiny.

Love, Dad

Sunday, January 19

Good Morning, Emily!

Crawl, Walk, Run: This is the natural order for how we learn and implement new ways of being. From learning to walk to mastering a new habit or hobby, we are destined to follow this intuitive instructional path. Some may think they are able to skip the first two steps, yet their initial success will be fraught with unnecessary challenges.

Love, Dad

Monday, January 20

Good Morning, Em!

Today is set aside to honor and remember Martin Luther King Jr., a flawed but noble man who unwillingly made the ultimate sacrifice for his beliefs and for our country. Growing up in the Northeast, I was not exposed to racial hate or discriminatory behavior. I was raised in an environment that believes all people are created equal. It was not until I lived in the South did I experience the harsh words of racial prejudice. To me, true racial prejudice, from any direction, displays ignorance and a lack of understanding. As humans, we are all equal in the eyes of our Creator.

Love, Dad

Tuesday January 21

Good Morning, Em!

Like most parents, your mother and I imparted upon you (and your brothers) the importance of speaking common courtesies, such as: "Please." "Thank you." "You're welcome." And addressing adults as "ma'am and sir." We were also taught to look others in the eye and lead with a proper handshake. Personal decency and proper etiquette should not escape us when we are unhappy, frustrated, or bored. These simple gestures cost nothing to employ yet seem like a forgotten art form for some of us.

Love, Dad

Good Morning, Emily!

Lead by example. I know over the years I have provided plenty of firsthand examples of good and poor behavior. Hopefully, you can learn from both, see past the latter, and embrace only the positive.

Love, Dad

Thursday, January 23

Good Morning, Sunshine!

Three simple life rules from Lou Holtz: "Do the right thing, do your best and show others you care."

Love, Dad

Friday, January 24

Good Morning, Em!

Don't let a few rocks in the road inhibit you from your intended journey.

Love, Dad

Saturday, January 25

Good Morning, Emily!

All decisions have consequences. While we want to avoid paralysis by analysis, one should consider the many possibilities and their corresponding consequences before acting. Clearly understand that not all choices can be easily reversed, if at all.

Love, Dad

P.S. If you're willing, I would be happy to talk to you about some of your decisions that you may be considering.

Sunday, January 26

Good Morning, Emily!

If you don't first succeed, do, do, and do it again.

Love, Dad

Monday, January 27

Good Morning, Em!

Be authentic, genuine, and real. We are all uniquely different and were created this way for a good reason. False facades and/or attempting to copy others is a waste of energy and only dilutes who you are. Like fine art, you are a masterpiece; no one wants to see the counterfeit copy.

Love, Dad

Tuesday, January 28

Good Morning, Sunshine!

Be a friend without an agenda. Be there, and try to anticipate what others need, whether it be it a kind word, offering a listening ear, or providing unwavering support. Just be there!

Love, Dad

Wednesday, January 29

Good Morning, Emily!

Focus on the journey, not the destination.

Love, Dad

Thursday, January 30

Good Morning, Em!

Procrastination did not cure the many horrible diseases, invent the mobile phone, or put a man on the moon. The act of procrastination is a lame excuse and a deep-rooted fear of failure. Push it aside and Do Better!

Love, Dad

Friday, January 31

Good Morning, Emily!

Wisdom is worth more than any amount of silver or gold, yet it is not something that we can buy off the shelve or order from Amazon.

Love, Dad

MONTH SIX
A HARD MESSAGE TO SHARE

ENTERING THE HALFWAY MARK of our journey, things seemed to be improving until we unexpectedly hit a wall as a family. It started in late January, where we observed an obvious change in Emily's demeanor. Attitudes shifted over a few weeks, which stirred conflict within the Holden household. Emotions began to run high and erratic, ultimately spilling over on to all in our home.

What sinister event could have displaced our progress? You guessed it—a new boyfriend. While a slight distraction, this added dynamic did bring some unintended consequences. Emily's conduct, and her disregard (or lack of empathy) for others within our home was pushing my wife and me to our wits' end. Something had to change, and quick.

This unwelcome terminus stop reminded me of a familiar quote by Richard Bach. "If you love someone, set them free. If they come back, they're yours; if they don't, they never were." Sadly, I was at the point where I was ready to set her free. Or evict her. I was emotionally torn between being a more than fed-up parent and a father wishing no harm would befall his child. The short-term solution was brutally open communication—and not the fun kind. The long-term solution established a departure deadline of June 1. For Emily, it would mean she needed to find permanent work and a future home. Regrettably, for me, it felt like we just took two steps backward.

Saturday, February 1

Good Morning, Sunshine!

Happiness is achieved through a life well lived with morals, faith, purpose, and reason.

Love, Dad

Sunday, February 2

Good Morning, Em!

Wisdom is like a guarded woman; she only bestows her presence upon you after you have experienced her through living.

Love, Dad

Monday, February 3

Good Morning, Em!

Sometimes all it takes to be strong and courageous is to acknowledge when you're wrong or to say sorry in a humble and sincere way. Owning what you've done takes more strength than making a clenched fist.

Love, Dad

Tuesday, February 4

Good Morning, Emily!

Love is the great equalizer in life; either being loved or loving another unconditionally, there is no substitute.

Love, Dad

Wednesday, February 5

Good Morning, Em!

Stop being passive, get out of the stands and onto the field of life. Fully engage, be present, and enjoy the gift of life that we have been given.

Love, Dad

Thursday, February 6

Good Morning, Emily!

You are smart. You are beautiful. You are strong! I am proud of you!

Love, Dad

Friday, February 7

Good Morning, Em!

"You will never do anything in this world without courage. It is the greatest quality of the mind next to honor."

—Aristotle

Love, Dad

Saturday, February 8

Good Morning, Em!

In any exchange with others, ask yourself, "What did I bring? What did I receive? and What am I grateful for?"

Love, Dad

(email in lieu of text)

Emily,

In light of our conversation this morning and your apparent inability to acknowledge how others are feeling, I could not simply send you a daily message without further context.

Today's message was going to be as follows.

Good Morning, Emily!

Don't let others steal your joy, and don't freely give it away.

Love, Dad

This is something that I wrote several days ago, and upon reflection of the events from this morning, I must amend my original thoughts to include the following:

And don't selfishly take away the joy from others.

Unfortunately, whether you can see it or not, your behavior is hurting your mother and me. At this point in our relationship, it can no longer be a one-way exchange. You are no longer a little girl who can simply shut down, hide away, and ignore your impact on those around you.

Your mother and I have provided you with everything, and more than most. And I am not only talking about material things. We are not perfect, yet we have provided you with an honorable example of what adults are expected to do and be in this world. We no longer owe you anything more than what has already been provided. If you wish to remain in our lives, you must be willing to step up, lose the victim mentality, own your behavior, and value our relationship.

I love you dearly, and that will never change, yet I am no longer willing to allow you to steal your mother's and my joy.

Love, Dad

Monday, February 10

Good Morning, Em!

Each and every new day gives us the opportunity to reflect, embrace our past, and start a brand-new chapter in our life. Have a better day than yesterday.

Love, Dad

Tuesday, February 11

Good Morning, Sunshine!

Two wise men once exclaimed,

"You can't always get what you want

But if you try sometime you find

You get what you need."

—Keith Richards & Mick Jagger

I know I have jested about this in the past, yet when reflecting on my life's experiences, I believe there's a lot of merit to their lyrics.

Love, Dad

Wednesday, February 12

Good Morning, Em!

A Vistage mate (Scott Love) recently shared a wise thought with me. He benefited by learning to "speak the other person's language"(see it through another's perspective by asking good questions and through active listening).

Love, Dad

Thursday, February 13

Good Morning, Emily!

Be willing to ask yourself and others hard questions, as that is the only way to get to the heart of the matter. Be wary of the easy answers as they tend to be veils.

Love, Dad

Friday, February 14

Good Morning, Emily!

Happy Valentine's Day!

Loving relationships will fill your heart and soul.

Love, Dad

Saturday, February 15

Good Morning, Em!

Confident and effective leaders hold themselves and others accountable and are honest and transparent about their intentions. They certainly do not act subversively or treat others in a sophomoric or passive aggressive manner. In addition to being disrespectful, the latter behaviors are a sign of immaturity and low EQ.

Love, Dad

Sunday, February 16

Good Morning, Em!

Receiving with gratitude and humility is a form of giving. Without gratitude there is no joy!

Love, Dad

Monday, February 17

Good Morning, Sunshine!

Today as a country we should celebrate President's Day! In lieu of a solemn observance and sincere appreciation of our Founding Fathers, we elect to have appliance and automotive sales. Most fail to recognize that this country's earliest patriots established the greatest governmental structure known to man. It's a shame that most of our recent past and current political leaders are only concerned about their own self-service, personal gain, and power. Thankfully, our Founding Fathers thought of more than just themselves.

Love, Dad

Tuesday, February 18

Good Morning, Em!

In lieu of electronic tribalism, seek the benefits of true communal relations.

Love, Dad

Wednesday, February 19

Good Morning, Emily!

To become a master of a skill, one must be focused on developing said skill, be willing to deliberately practice, be good with struggle and sacrifice, and do much more than simply put in the time.

Love, Dad

Thursday, February 20

Good Morning, Em!

In life's situations where you may be unable to directly influence the end result of a matter, you still have the ability to affect how you show up when dealing with it.

Love, Dad

Friday, February 21

Good Morning, Emily!

Innovation is a new way of doing old things. It's the result of collaboration and sharing of ideas. Don't fear any risk, change, and/or the possibility of failure associated with innovation.

Love, Dad

Saturday, February 22

Good Morning, Em!

"I was gonna!" is not an actionable statement. Do yourself a favor and drop that phrase (and excuse) from your vocabulary.

Love, Dad

Sunday, February 23

Good Morning, Sunshine!

"Life without intention is like a boat without a rudder."

—Todd Musselman

Love, Dad

Monday, February 24

Good Morning, Emily!

"We are what we repeatedly do. Excellence, then, is not an act, but a habit."

—Aristotle

Love, Dad

Tuesday, February 25

Good Morning, Emily!

How do you show up and see yourself in the future? One of the interesting things about us humans is our ability to envision the future, specifically the outcome of future events or possibilities as we wish them to occur. The key is having the tenacity, conviction, and grit to see the results as envisioned through to their end means.

Love, Dad

Wednesday, February 26

Good Morning, Em!

If you cannot lead yourself, you cannot lead others.

Love, Dad

Thursday, February 27

Good Morning, Emily!

Sticks and stones may break your bones, yet pure stupidity can certainly kill you.

Love, Dad

Good Morning, Em!

Know that not everyone in the world has a good heart like you. Regrettably, there are hurtful people in this world who do not have your best interests at heart. As time passes, these individuals will be easier to spot and step around.

Love, Dad

Good Morning, Sunshine!

Happy Leap Day!

"There is nothing on this earth more to prized than true friendship."

—Thomas Aquinas

Leap Day = Free Day, so make the very most of this gift.

Love, Dad

MONTH SEVEN
ADDED CHALLENGE

DESPITE THE OVERWHELMING AMOUNT of information at our fingertips, no one saw the coronavirus (COVID-19) coming. COVID-19 and its effects on the general population obviously caught everyone by surprise. I was deeply saddened by the loss of life and the aftermath caused by this virus. I was also frustrated by the unprecedented reaction and overwhelming impact this disease had on our nation. At the time of my writing this (April 2020), I sincerely hope the imposed solutions are not worse than the disease. Meaning, I hope the shutting down of our nation does not have more unintended consequences that significantly stretch beyond the actual effects of the disease. Currently, it is too soon to know.

Like most, the Holden family hunkered down. Soon we were all together under one roof, healthy and safe. Our sons returned home from college for spring break and would not return for the semester. Understandably, COVID-19 had dissolved the previous months' trepidations. Maybe a silver lining to a very dark storm cloud.

Thankfully, in our part of the world, the construction industry was deemed an essential business. While we had to make many adjustments to the rapidly changing requirements, I truly felt blessed to be able to work. Millions were not as fortunate. Truly, a sad state of affairs for our country. I am confident that the people of our great nation will overcome this invisible enemy.

As time passed, I tried to tailor my daily messages to offset the nonstop wave of negativity. I wanted to provide hope and guidance without calling attention to the obvious. Because it was a very strange and unprecedented time, it was my hope that these simple statements would break through the turbulence of anxiety and fear. Only time will tell.

Sunday, March 1

Good Morning, Emily!

Do not discard the faith instilled in you at a younger age. Heed the advice of an older man who struggles to make sense, wondering what he may have missed as he searches for spiritual fulfillment.

Love, Dad

Monday, March 2

Good Morning, Em!

Work to build thicker skin, and do not take everything personally. Know that many things will be directed toward you that need to simply roll off your back. Offer these thornless barbs no acknowledgement.

Love, Dad

Tuesday, March 3

Good Morning, Sunshine!

Have a strong heart. While we never want it to happen, know that someone or something will break it. This pain may seem earth-shattering at the time, yet it's healthy emotional pain that will soon subside.

Love, Dad

Wednesday, March 4

Good Morning, Em!

"Tell me and I forget. Teach me and I remember. Involve me and I learn."

—Benjamin Franklin

What is the one thing you wish I had shared with you when you were an adolescent girl?

Love, Dad

Thursday, March 5

Good Morning, Emily!

Convictions are the jet fuel that powers our progress, whereas out-of-control emotions can act as a drag chute.

Love, Dad

Friday, March 6

Good Morning, Sunshine!

Successful people look for new ways to solve old problems—as opposed to dropping problems at the feet of others.

Love, Dad

Saturday, March 7

Good Morning, Em!

Pick yourself up. Do not look for (or expect) others to lift you up when you are struggling, fall down, or fail.

Love, Dad

Sunday, March 8

Good Morning, Emily!

Share enthusiastically, but do not give away your joy!

Love, Dad

Monday, March 9

Good Morning, Emily!

Don't opt out of life in exchange for victimization or the ultimate pursuit of extreme self-esteem.

Love, Dad

Tuesday, March 10

Good Morning, Em!

Always honor your word and do what you said you would do without hesitation—even when no one else is looking.

Love, Dad

Wednesday, March 11

Good Morning, Em!

The harsh reality and fact is that the world owes us nothing in life. There are no guarantees of success. You will get out of life exactly what you put into it.

Love, Dad

Thursday, March 12

Good Morning, Emily!

Do not go through life with hidden agendas. Be true to yourself and act with humility and grace.

Love, Dad

Friday, March 13

Good Morning, Sunshine!

Having confidence in one's own worth, abilities, and personal self-respect is extremely important. However extreme self-esteem propped up by the constant need for others to affirm our worth, confirming that we are special, is unhealthy and prideful. Have command over your self-esteem; do not blindly rely on others for this evaluation.

Love, Dad

Saturday, March 14

Good Morning, Em!

It is unwise to apply current-day beliefs, cultural norms, and sensibilities to the past. The past shall remain in the past. We should learn from it and not try to alter it based upon our newly formed biases and beliefs.

Love, Dad

Sunday, March 15

Good Morning, Emily!

"Giving is living."

—Morrie Schwartz

The act of helping others and/or an act of kindness is a natural human expression that, when consistency practiced, helps to make us more complete.

Love, Dad

Monday, March 16

Good Morning, Sunshine!

Life's uncertainties will come in many forms. Don't fall prey to a fatalistic or scarcity mindset. Like all other animals, our brains are hardwired to identify threats. Thus, we tend to act irrationally in the face of uncertainty. In the absence of information, we have two choices: 1) we can allow negativity and darkness to creep in, or 2) we can allow the light in and let positivity sterilize our negative emotions. Personally, I choose the light.

Love, Dad

Tuesday, March 17

Good Morning, Emily!

We all have things that "appear" to work against us, but in time, the fog of uncertainty will fade, and the truth will prevail. Ultimately, with some effort, you can find the success and happiness that you may be seeking.

Love, Dad

Wednesday, March 18

Good Morning, Em!

If you cannot see yourself in the vision of the future that you desire, you won't be able to get out of your own way.

Love, Dad

Thursday, March 19

Good Morning, Sunshine!

There will be things throughout your life that are worth fighting for. If there is something in this world that you truly want, be willing to fight for it. In this context, "fight" does not equate to aggression or violence, it refers to your personal level of perseverance combined with a balanced degree of assertiveness.

Love, Dad

Friday, March 20

Good Morning, Em!

Money: Some wrongfully believe it will bring happiness, and others feel it's the root of all evil. Simply, it's a resource and a tool. Like all resources, it has its limits and shouldn't be squandered. And like all tools, it should be used in the correct manner for its intended purpose and properly maintained.

Love, Dad

Good Morning, Em!

Why is it that most of our what-if? imaginations seem to have negative outcomes? For example, *What if I try something new and I struggle or fail?* Instead, consider, *What if I don't go for it and I later regret it?* We have control over our what-ifs? so why not make them optimistic and positive.

Love, Dad

Good Morning, Emily!

The value of hope: We as humans require a steady diet of love and hope. There is an expectation that the future will be brighter. We often yearn for somebody or something, an outcome that is not easily obtainable. Hope is the desire that something good will happen. Maintaining hope creates a positive energy that raises our spirits. So, it seems, hope is the light we require. It is in our best interest to never, ever lose hope!

Love, Dad

Monday, March 23

Good Morning, Sunshine!

You will never grow to your full potential living in a fear-based world. Whether it be a fear of failure, the fear of not being liked, the fear of not getting along with others, or the fear of the unknown, it's imperative to stop "what-iffing?" your every decision.

Love, Dad

Tuesday, March 24

Good Morning, Em!

In life we are meant to continually learn, improve, and expand our personal abilities.

Use this abundance of idle time to expand your mind; it will only make you stronger.

"Once you stop learning, you start dying."

—Albert Einstein

Love, Dad

Wednesday, March 25

Good Morning, Em!

Serving others by helping them become a better leader is more fulfilling than the construction of any building and creates a greater impact far into the future.

Love, Dad

Thursday, March 26

Good Morning, Emily!

Fun, fair, and positive sports where everyone wins and everyone gets a trophy was a generational misstep for our culture. This extreme self-esteem unbalance wrongfully robbed a generation of the life lessons associated with losing, struggle, and the value of perseverance.

Love, Dad

Friday, March 27

Good Morning, Em!

Others see what we do not. Having someone else hold a mirror up to identify our blind spots is a must, and we regularly need the discerning eyes of others to humble us; therefore, seek out the appraisal of others. Feedback is a gift. When received, actively listen and simply say thank you.

Love, Dad

Saturday, March 28

Good Morning, Sunshine!

When serving others, do not engage in the use of decaying or corrupting words. Only communicate using purposeful words of encouragement that build up the recipient.

Love, Dad

Sunday, March 29

Good Morning, Emily!

While we are all inherently unique as individuals, this doesn't free us from the challenges in life. What empowers us to step boldly into the world is our ability to overcome said challenges; it's our approach to adversity; it's our drive to set ourselves apart through our own efforts and not through the actions or words of others.

Love, Dad

Monday, March 30

Good Morning, Em!

"Attitude ... I'm convinced that life is 10 percent what happens to you and 90 percent how you react to it."

—Charles R. Swindoll

Love, Dad

P.S. It may seem counterintuitive, yet more now than before, you will benefit from hustling and applying for jobs and looking for opportunities. Saying, "What's the use?" is only going to put you behind the other sheep.

Tuesday, March 31

Good Morning, Sunshine!

Managing stress and anxiety—be it from personal constraints, work, or resulting from matters beyond our control—is paramount to our health and success. Regular sleep, a healthy diet, exercise, deep breathing, meditation, and prayer are just a few things you can do to maintain an even keel.

Love, Dad

MONTH EIGHT
THIS IS HARDER THAN IT LOOKS

A little more than halfway through my texting journey, I began to realize that it is not easy coming up with original material every day. Producing almost four hundred uplifting, motivating, or thought-provoking messages is not an easy task. In January, when I cemented my resolution, I did not fully consider the magnitude of my commitment before embarking on this endeavor. Doubts about my preparedness to see this through to its end destination were intensifying.

As I looked to the world around me for inspiration, I also started to question my own motives and integrity. Hoping that I was not emulating the spirit of a nagging or lecturing father, internal questions bubbled to the surface. *Are my efforts to share some of life's wisdom (as I see it) helpful or engaging?* And, *Will my words have the desired effect, or are they simply the ramblings of a bitter old man?* Only Emily would be able to answer these questions.

In the course of my search, I found myself recording personal observations or quips like Andy Rooney. I started to feel like an old curmudgeon, venting and providing personal insights about current affairs and other worldly events. Mr. Rooney's opening trademark statement, "Did you ever wonder why … ?" darted randomly across my mind like a fly looking for its next meal. Resolved to do better, I pressed onward.

During this same period of doubt, I began to wonder if my words were unwantedly falling on deaf ears. My wife was quick to remind me of why I chose to pursue this tactic, and it was not for an instant reply. Satisfied with her answer, I regrouped and doubled down with the end goal in mind.

While some of my observations may have tones of an old, grouchy commentator, the daily messages within this book are my own thoughts. Equally, they represent my own personal opinions, beliefs, and colorful commentary on life as I see it. In some instances, that was still not always enough, and I struggled to find the right words. This caused me to seek out others for help.

Disclaimer: Apart from expressly identified quotations from much smarter people and the recycled comments made by my family, close friends, colleagues, and some random strangers, the passages within are my own and may be an irritant for some. If this is the case for you, the reader should consult the following messages: Wednesday, December 11; Wednesday, April 15; Thursday, May 14; and Tuesday, May 17 for further direction and clarification.

Good Morning, Emily!

Akin to the melting spring snow transitioning to runoff and a winding river that eventually makes its way to the sea, "This too shall pass." This Persian proverb reminds us that all events, bad or good, naturally run their course.

Love, Dad

Good Morning, Em!

Recognize the crucible moments within your life. These profound events help to shape, change, and forge who we are as individuals and will often alter the course of one's life.

Love, Dad

Good Morning, Emily!

Learn to trust your gut. Your instinctual feelings are usually right, so when your gut sends your brain notifications, heed their messages.

Love, Dad

Saturday, April 4

Good Morning, Sunshine!

Meet nonphysical aggression (hostile attitudes or incivility) with grace and love. These humble gestures are very disarming, which can evoke an equally humble result.

Love, Dad

Sunday, April 5

Good Morning, Em!

"If you judge people, you have no time to love them."

—Mother Teresa

Love, Dad

Monday, April 6

Good Morning, Emily!

Confident and effective leaders hold themselves accountable first. Accountability must start in the mirror long before looking for others to hold them accountable.

Love, Dad

Tuesday, April 7

Good Morning, Em!

Despite what you may believe, the road to success is not a linear pathway. It is, in fact, a curvy, mixed-up succession of unpredictable steps. Sometimes we must go backward to go forward. While it may appear counterintuitive, don't be afraid to take these uncomfortable steps.

Love, Dad

Wednesday, April 8

Good Morning, Emily!

Know that when things may seem the darkest, the light and confidence you require to beat any obstacle is within you.

Love, Dad

Thursday, April 9

Good Morning, Sunshine!

"Nothing ventured, nothing gained. You can't get anywhere unless you're willing to take a risk."

—Geoffrey Chaucer

Love, Dad

Friday, April 10

Good Morning, Em!

When receiving feedback, avoid the three Ds: deflect, deny, and defend. Actively listen, then simply say thank you to ensure the feedback continues.

Love, Dad

Saturday, April 11

Good Morning, Emily!

Summon your curiosity and explore. Strike out and foster the sweetness that comes from inspiration and creativity.

Love, Dad

Good Morning, Sunshine, and Happy Easter!

For many of faith, today is a day to celebrate the resurrection of Jesus Christ, the sacrifice he made, and the birth of a new beginning. Within ourselves, we have the opportunity every day to resurrect new ways of living and being. As individuals we must own how we approach those possibilities.

Have faith in your own ability to resurrect yourself.

"Live as if you were to die tomorrow. Learn as if you were to live forever."

—Mahatma Gandhi

Love, Dad

Good Morning, Em!

Good friend, wise man, and fellow coworker J. Eric Martin once shared with me a saying his father told him when he was growing up: "Old too soon, smart too late." Simply put, we do not understand and appreciate the wisdom of life until we are too old.

Love, Dad

Tuesday, April 14

Good Morning, Emily!

During this very sad and tragic time in our country's history, we cannot fail to remember those who sacrificed more for the greater good of others.

Love, Dad

Wednesday, April 15

Good Morning, Emily!

"Be who you are and say what you feel. Because those who mind, don't matter. And those who matter, don't mind!"

—Dr. Seuss

Love, Dad

P.S. I'm grateful for the opportunity to talk last night. I realize that it was about an uncomfortable subject, and I did more of the talking, yet I appreciated that you were willing to listen. Have a better day!

Thursday, April 16

Good Morning, Em!

Mea Culpa: Acknowledge when you are wrong, at fault, or have made a mistake. Don't be the victim or pass blame when the error falls squarely at your feet.

Love, Dad

Friday, April 17

Good Morning, Emily!

From my own experiences, I've learned the hard way that one must think through decisions and foresee the results before acting on them. I'm certainly not endorsing paralysis by analysis; I just want you to understand the risks and repercussions for all parties involved. I should also add that once you do have a decision, go forward with confidence.

Love, Dad

Saturday, April 18

Good Morning, Sunshine!

Both John D. Rockefeller and later Jim Collins had it correct when they proclaimed, respectively, "Don't be afraid to give up the good to go for the great," and "Good is the enemy of great." In short, don't settle for mediocrity or good enough; strive for something much more.

Love, Dad

Good Morning, Em!

Love is the only act that truly endures the distance and test of time.

Love, Dad

Good Morning, Sunshine!

"The children now love luxury; they have bad manners, contempt for authority; they show disrespect for elders and love chatter in place of exercise. Children are now tyrants, not the servants of their households. They no longer rise when elders enter the room. They contradict their parents, chatter before company, gobble up dainties at the table, cross their legs, and tyrannize their teachers."

—Socrates

Wow! Talk about having the ability to predict the future. It's amazing how not much has changed over nearly 125 generations. This is where you would say "Okay, Boomer!" (even though I'm a Gen Xer). If it's any comfort to you, I'm sure parents 125 generations from now will be muttering the same assertions under their breath.

Love, Dad

Tuesday, April 21

Good Morning, Emily!

The only visions that take hold are shared visions. Invest in getting others to see your vision for the future; it's the only way for it to come true.

It's your grandfather's birthday today!

Love, Dad

Wednesday, April 22

Good Morning, Emily!

Take time to celebrate the successes in life. Even the ones that may seem insignificant. Too often, in a blind march to "get things done," I haven't stopped to acknowledge these incredibly important events.

Love, Dad

Thursday, April 23

Good Morning, Em!

Under-commit and over-deliver. Some view this as sandbagging or being too conservative. The recipients (and you) of this strategy will ultimately benefit and appreciate this proactive approach.

Love, Dad

Good Morning, Sunshine!

"Aim small, miss small." While this maxim is mostly attributed to shooting or hunting, it can be applied to other parts of our life. It's okay to aim for larger goals, yet make sure your targets are in focus and you fully understand what lies behind them.

Love, Dad

Saturday, April 25

Good Morning, Em!

Why is it that some of our missteps in life seem to play out in a slow-motion crash and burn? Maybe it's life's way of making sure we experience the pain of our failures with our eyes wide open.

Love, Dad

Sunday, April 26

Good Morning, Emily!

Practicing kindness is the root to many admired qualities.

"Kindness in words creates confidence. Kindness in thinking creates profoundness. Kindness in giving creates love."

—Lao Tzu

Love, Dad

Monday, April 27

Good Morning, Emily!

"Coming together is a beginning; keeping together is progress; working together is success."

—Henry Ford

This quotation reinforces the power and capability of a united team. Strive to Do Better! through the participation in and leadership of high-performing teams.

Love, Dad

Tuesday, April 28

Good Morning, Em!

While our safety is paramount, I'm concerned with the potential effects and implementation of social distancing during this pandemic. We cannot lose what binds us together as humans. Face-to-face interaction is extremely important for our well-being. Hopefully, these temporary remedies do not turn into long-term behavioral norms.

Love, Dad

Good Morning, Em!

"Courage has nothing to do with our determination to be great. It has to do with what we decide in that moment when we are called upon to be more."

—Rita Dove

Love, Dad

Good Morning, Emily!

Owen recently shared this quote with me regarding the reality surrounding our eroding liberties. Unfortunately, it seems all too true, especially in the light of recent events.

"History teaches that grave threats to liberty often come in times of urgency, when constitutional rights seem too extravagant to endure."

—Thurgood Marshall

Love, Dad

MONTH NINE
THE ROAD TO RECOVERY

Entering the eighth week of the COVID-19 pandemic, the American psyche is straining from the pull between fear and freedom. Now on the so-called "road to recovery," the "new normal" brought face masks, social distancing, and reduced personal interaction. Regrettably, a new pastime of public shaming by some for not following in lockstep with the timid among us was in practice.

Many, like me, became disenfranchised with the ongoing governmental overreach of our liberties. The masks seemed to be an attempt to silence our rights and voices. Overnight, we went from a vibrant economy to tens of millions who are out of work, with many being plunged back into poverty. Only history will tell if we chose correctly as a nation. I fear our overzealous actions have only added to our country's heartache and suffering.

It makes me wonder how earlier generations like the "Greatest Generation" would have reacted under the same constraint. My gut tells me that they would not have done the same. A generation that witnessed the loss of 70–85 million people caused by the war, war-related disease, and famine must be turning over in their graves. While extremely frustrated, I still hold hope in my heart that the American spirit will overcome this challenge and its people will persevere.

Good Morning, Em!

There are two sides to every story, and the truth lies somewhere in the middle. Take the time to properly inform yourself before acting on any one story or another, even if one is your own.

Love, Dad

Good Morning, Sunshine!

Don't allow a natural negativity basis to creep in. If fostered, it will grow like a kudzu vine, invading until it smothers all hope of optimism and possibility.

Love, Dad

Sunday, May 3

Good Morning, Emily!

Values matter! Live your life with Integrity, Humility, Honor, Respect, Loyalty, Grace, and a Good Heart.

Love, Dad

Monday, May 4

Good Morning, Emily!

"No one can make you feel inferior without your consent."

—Eleanor Roosevelt

Love, Dad

Tuesday, May 5

Good Morning, Em!

Don't fall prey to thinking, "I'll be happy when ..." Seek happiness in all that you do. As well, put firm limits on self-pity, especially when life hands you unhappy events. Find solace in the fact that it often will, and act with grace when it does.

Love, Dad

Wednesday, May 6

Good Morning, Emily!

Children are a great equalizer. They will provide calm for someone who is uptight, provide clarity for those of us who lack focus, organization for those of us who are in chaos, and smooth out the edges for those of us who are jagged. Of course, they will also provide the corresponding results for those with the opposing afflictions.

Love, Dad

Thursday, May 7

Good Morning, Emily!

In my youth, I spent many years in the Scouts. I learned several life skills and values that served me well. Upon reflection, I can solemnly state that the oath below still rings true today.

"On my honor, I will do my best to do my duty to God and my country and to obey the Scout Law;

to help other people at all times; to keep myself physically strong, mentally awake and morally straight."

—Boy Scout Oath

Love, Dad

Good Morning, Emily!

Play by the rules of life. We are human. We make errors, and some of us will receive needed penalties. However, stop assessing yourself unearned penalties, and don't disqualify yourself from the game of life. Go boldly out into the world and compete like it's your final race.

Love, Dad

Good Morning, Em!

In challenging times, leaders look for new solutions that will make their team, or company, stronger.

Love, Dad

Sunday, May 10

Good Morning, Emily!

Today is Mother's Day.

You, like your brothers, were blessed with your mother's personality. With a big heart, she is always selflessly looking after the needs of others before her own. Take every opportunity to exhibit these traits, as they will best serve you and others around you.

It should go without saying that we should never fail to remember or celebrate our mothers. Be very thankful for the life she gave you.

Love, Dad

Monday, May 11

Good Morning, Em!

Celebrate the small wins in your life. Don't wait for the huge milestones to stop and take notice. Enjoy your and other's efforts along the journey.

Love, Dad

Tuesday, May 12

Good Morning, Emily!

If someone wants to offer you feedback, be an active listener. Don't respond, argue, or feel as if you need to reply with a justification. Just be quiet. When they are done, simply say thank you. Once you have the feedback, you can digest it, reflect upon it, and later act on it. However, when in the moment, just absorb it and understand that feedback is a gift.

Love, Dad

Wednesday, May 13

Good Morning, Emily!

Anyone who has claimed they have never lied is lying. We all struggle with this act, especially when it comes to telling little white lies. Fundamentally, it is a wayward path, as no one is able to keep up with all the stories they have told. It's just best to stick with the truth, especially when it's going to hurt.

Love, Dad

Thursday, May 14

Good Morning, Em!

While the First Amendment of the Constitution protects from "abridging the freedom of speech," it doesn't protect us from being offended by the speech of others. We struggle today as a society, as we cannot honestly say what we truly feel out of fear of reprisals. These unsavory repercussions fly directly in the face of our Founding Fathers, their fundamental beliefs, and our rights. In short, with conviction and decency, speak up about topics that you're passionate and informed about.

Love, Dad

Friday, May 15

Good Morning, Sunshine!

Always work hard and put forth your very best effort. Never ask someone else to do something that you're not willing to do. Treat people how you want to be treated.

Love, Dad

Saturday, May 16

Good Morning, Emily!

Only you have the control to put forth the level of effort needed to achieve your goals. No one else can do it for you. Never back down on effort. When you think you've done enough, do a little more. It's very rare to put forth too much effort.

Love, Dad

Sunday, May 17

Good Morning, Em!

"Great minds discuss ideas; average minds discuss events; small minds discuss people."

—Eleanor Roosevelt

Love, Dad

Monday, May 18

Good Morning, Em!

It is unhealthy to seek validation and affirmation online. These vital social cues should result from close personal exchanges, relationships, and from within, ideally from trusted friends and family.

Love, Dad

Tuesday, May 19

Good Morning, Em!

Being naturally or automatically offended by every response or comment is not a normal reflex. For some people, responding negatively has been turned into a pastime, an art form, and an occupation. This is surprising, because it takes more effort and energy to be negative.

Love, Dad

Wednesday, May 20

Good Morning, Emily!

When did we become so entitled? (Entitlement is the feeling of having a right to something, inherently deserving of privileges or special treatment.) And why are so many in society becoming offended due to a sense of entitlement? I don't remember this being voted on or passed into law, yet just the fact that I am asking these questions will trigger someone's narcissistic alarm, causing me to be labeled as insensitive.

Love, Dad

Thursday, May 21

Good Morning, Em!

It's best to learn to humble yourself and not wait for others to do it for you.

Love, Dad

Friday, May 22

Good Morning, Sunshine!

The Serenity Prayer has been used by many in an effort to build the strength needed to forge through difficult times. Honestly, these words have aided me more times than I can count.

"God, grant me the serenity to accept the things I cannot change, courage to change the things I can, and wisdom to know the difference."

—Karl Paul Reinhold Niebuhr

Love, Dad

Saturday, May 23

Good Morning, Emily!

"Experience is a hard teacher because she gives the test first, the lesson afterward."

—Vernon Law

Love, Dad

Sunday, May 24

Good Morning, Em!

Reach deep within your personal fortitude for the strength to walk through the invisible walls of anxiety and fear that are propped up in your mind. Shatter any perceived glass ceiling that may be holding you down. Know that if you wish to have peace and happiness in your life, you have to let it in.

Love, Dad

Monday, May 25

Good Morning, Emily!

Memorial Day is a very solemn day. Most fail to pause and truly reflect upon the sacrifice of the few for the benefit of the many. We are indebted to those great Americans who laid their life on the altar of freedom. President Ronald Regan summed it up well when he stated, "Freedom is never more than one generation away from extinction. We didn't pass it to our children in the bloodstream. It must be fought for, protected, and handed on for them to do the same." With this in mind, ask yourself, "Who or what am I willing to fight (and possibly die) for?"

Love, Dad

Tuesday, May 26

Good Morning, Emily!

The wrong people will be quick to pull you down, and the right people will always help lift you up.

Love, Dad

Wednesday, May 27

Good Morning, Em!

The most meaningful and straightforward way to lift someone else's spirits can be expressed by saying simple phrases, such as, "Thank you!", "I appreciate you!" or "I love you!"

Love, Dad

Thursday, May 28

Good Morning, Em!

True servant leaders will express their appreciation of others through genuine gratitude and authenticity.

Love, Dad

Good Morning, Emily!

With great power comes an even greater responsibility for a leader to ensure that all members of the team are being served long before the leaders needs are even considered.

Love, Dad

Good Morning, Sunshine!

As humans, we are not meant to be idle. There is dignity and purpose in work, yet so many put more energy into avoiding it than the effort needed to accomplish what is being avoided. An unwanted task done well is better than a worthy task done poorly.

Love, Dad

Sunday, May 31

Good Morning, Emily,

"We but mirror the world. All the tendencies present in the outer world are to be found in the world of our body. If we could change ourselves, the tendencies in the world would also change. As a man changes his own nature, so does the attitude of the world change towards him. This is the divine mystery supreme. A wonderful thing it is and the source of our happiness. We need not wait to see what others do."

—Mahatma Gandhi

Love, Dad

MONTH TEN
LOOMING DEADLINE

IN EARLY FEBRUARY 2020, we (my wife and I) decided that the first of June was an acceptable departure deadline. This strategy provided Emily with just over three months to figure out her plan to exit the nest and our home. Despite COVID-19 and the turmoil it created, Emily honored our agreement. On the morning of her planned departure, Emily had her car pre-packed to the ceiling with all her worldly possessions and best friend in tow. She was off. With a proper Colorado send-off (two inches of unexpected snow), my little girl headed east to Illinois.

Honestly, it was a bittersweet departure. While I was sad to see her go, we knew that it was time for her to start her own life. We all require autonomy, the opportunity to be the master and maker of our own rules. She was no different. Unfortunately, COVID-19 created an added level of complexity and stress for this transition. Pandemic be damned, this was still the logical and best move for our family. In time, I hoped Emily would agree.

The rest of the month of June was quiet. Besides sending my daily messages, which remained mostly one-directional, our one-to-one communication was limited to a Father's Day phone call and a few utilitarian texts. Frankly, this was most likely for the best (and possibly therapeutic), as we all needed some time to decompress and adjust to our new environments.

Monday, June 1

Good Morning, Emily!

Similar to justice, empathy must be applied equally, fairly, without bias, and with love.

Love, Dad

Tuesday, June 2

Good Morning, Em!

Our life will be out of balance until we are able to come to terms with who we really are. This does not mean giving up on one's hopes or dreams; in fact, it's just the opposite. It is simply easier to obtain our desired results once we draw from the knowledge and confidence of true self-awareness.

Love, Dad

Wednesday, June 3

Good Morning, Emily!

Life would be too simple (and boring) if we had the ability to "will" our more challenging beliefs or desires into immediate actions and results.

Love, Dad

Thursday, June 4

Good Morning, Em!

Learn to manage your temperament. How we show up is 100 percent within your control.

Love, Dad

Friday, June 5

Good Morning, Sunshine!

There is no such thing as a risk-free, effort-free, issue-free, or conflict-free existence. There will always be rocks in the road for us to navigate around.

Love, Dad

Saturday, June 6

Good Morning, Em!

Today is the 76th anniversary of D-Day. Just five days prior to this historic event, your grandfather, James J. Goebel Jr., walked across the French border into Switzerland and became an allied evadee after forty-five days on the run. He was safely smuggled through the Belgium and French underground after being shot down while returning from an inaugural bombing mission over Germany. Many Patriots (Resistance members) risked their lives, with some perishing in the process. We cannot forget that millions sacrificed much more than we are right now and, thankfully, freedom prevails as a result.

Love, Dad

Sunday, June 7

Good Morning, Emily!

It's okay to be scared about some unknowns in life, yet do not allow that interpretation paralyze you from moving forward.

"Fear isn't an excuse to come to a standstill, it's the impetus to step up and strike."

—Arthur Ashe

Love, Dad

Monday, June 8

Good Morning, Em!

Leaving home, you will now truly begin to grow into your own as an adult. Do so with the confidence that you have much to offer. You are a smart and beautiful woman made of good values and strong stock. Go forward into to the world with wind in your wings, the sun on your back, and the knowledge that you are loved.

Love, Dad

Tuesday, June 9

Good Morning, Emily!

Today you are embarking on a new chapter within your life. Your mother and I have provided you with the roots needed to build upon. We wish great success, happiness, and safe travels along your journey. Going forward, it's all in your hands and actions. Now that you are using your wings, you will have the autonomy to live your life as you see fit. Have confidence in your choices to make the best decisions and in your ability to Do Better! We love you!

P.S. This morning's snowy send-off is Mother Nature's subtle reminder that we should always expect the unexpected. This is what makes life so exciting.

Love, Dad

Wednesday, June 10

Good Morning, Emily!

"Change has a considerable psychological impact on the human mind. To the fearful it is threatening because it means that things may get worse. To the hopeful it is encouraging because things may get better. To the confident it is inspiring because the challenge exists to make things better."

—King Whitney Jr.

Love, Dad

Thursday, June 11

Good Morning, Em!

Music helps us to recall events in time, memories of friends, special feelings, and moments in life. For me, just a snippet of lyrics can trigger thoughts of a dear friend who passed away a year ago today.

"Forget your lust for the rich man's gold, all that you need is in your soul"

—from the song "Simple Man" by Lynyrd Skynyrd

Love, Dad

Good Morning, Sunshine!

Won't vs. Can't: As you know, one of my least favorite phases is "I can't." To me, it personifies an unwillingness to even try or to put effort into something that is within your ability. "I won't" clearly implies you will not do something. I prefer the latter statement, as it's an honest response.

Love, Dad

Good Morning, Em!

Fear of the unknown will not move me forward. Faith and positive energy most certainly will.

Love, Dad

Good Morning, Emily!

Today is Flag Day!

On this day, "Old Glory" should be celebrated and honored with a pledge. From the beginning, our countrymen have laid their lives at the altar of freedom for this cloth. Freedom is represented by three colors. Red symbolizes hardiness and valor; white symbolizes purity and innocence; and blue represents vigilance, perseverance, and justice. America's stars and stripes are indelible, her colors may fade, yet they will never run.

Love, Dad

Good Morning, Em!

The Stockdale Paradox

"You must never confuse the need for absolute unwavering faith that you can and will prevail in the end with the discipline to confront the brutal facts of your reality."

—Jim Collins

Love, Dad

Tuesday, June 16

Good Morning, Emily!

I've made a lot of mistakes in my life. You will not
inherit these, nor are you destined to follow in my
footsteps. You are destined to make your own mistakes.
How you learn, grow, and move forward from these
experiences will truly shape who you become—not
some predetermined destiny based on the past. Believe
in yourself and your own ability to navigate through
these challenges. Ultimately, you will take action or an
alternative course.

Love, Dad

Wednesday, June 17

Good Morning, Em!

Looking for simple solutions to complex problems will
mostly lead you astray. The answers to these challenges
can be frustrating, yet they will arrive sooner with
more than one mind focused on them.

Love, Dad

Thursday, June 18

Good Morning, Em!

The best things in life don't come easy. Be willing to tackle the more difficult challenges, and don't shy away from the roads less traveled. Openly embrace the Herculean effort.

Love, Dad

Friday, June 19

Good Morning, Emily,

Constantly labeling oneself negatively through self-doubt or assigning self-blame will only ensure less-than-favorable results.

Love, Dad

Saturday, June 20

Good Morning, Em!

Don't look for or wait on the empty validation from social media to fulfill you. Fulfillment comes from real relationships, which are sometimes difficult and complex, yet they are absolutely worth the effort and time.

Love, Dad

Sunday, June 21

Good Morning, Emily!

"If you cannot find peace within yourself, you will never find it anywhere else."

—Marvin Gaye

Have a peaceful day.

Love, Dad

Footnote: When I selected today's quote, I was unaware of the tragedy behind Marvin Gaye's death. Ironically and sadly, he was shot by his father while trying to break up a fight between his parents. A father at the time of his death, Marvin was survived by his three children.

Monday, June 22

Good Morning, Emily!

Do not succumb to superfluous push notifications from disingenuous external distractions. Learn to separate yourself from the never-ending loop of these calls to attention.

Love, Dada

Tuesday, June 23

Good Morning, Emily!

Fight for what you believe in, and never sit idly by waiting for others to lead. Lead with good intent and for positive change.

Love, Dad

Wednesday, June 24

Good Morning, Em!

"I used to think communication was key until I realized comprehension is. You can communicate all you want to someone, but if they don't understand you, it won't reach them the way you need it to."

—Unknown

Love, Dad

Thursday, June 25

Good Morning, Em!

When it comes to decision making, true leaders will remain impartial, balanced, and will have the courage to make the unpopular decision. In doing so, these leaders will obtain success by upholding team integrity and trust.

Love, Dad

Good Morning, Sunshine!

Never harbor resentment or go to bed angry. Doing so will only invite sour dreams, a restless night, and will carry negativity into another day.

Love, Dad

Saturday, June 27

Good Morning, Em!

KISS Principle: Keep It Simple Stupid. Thanks to the US Navy and its plethora of acronyms, we are reminded that systems work best when we don't overcomplicate the design (or life) and keep things simple.

Love, Dad

Sunday, June 28

Good Morning, Emily!

Live to your full potential. Stop reacting to your life and take control of it. Be intentional and own it!

"The most difficult thing is the decision to act. The rest is merely tenacity."

—Amelia Earhart

Love, Dad

Monday, June 29

Good Morning, Emily!

"The most important person we will ever manage is ourselves. You cannot lead others until you manage yourself."

—Allen Hauge

Love, Dad

Tuesday, June 30

Good Morning Em!

In a speech, Nicholas Murray Butler stated, "The vast population of this earth, and indeed nations themselves, may readily be divided into three groups. There are the few who make things happen, the many more who watch things happen, and the overwhelming majority who have no notion of what happens. Every human being is born into this third and largest group; it is for himself, his environment and his education to determine whether he shall rise to the second group or even to the first." So, which group will you strive to be in?

Love, Dad

MONTH ELEVEN
DIGGING DEEPER

REGRETFULLY, THERE WAS LITTLE interaction with my daughter after her departure from home. Other than a couple of brief conversations, life was relatively quiet. I am not sure if this was the result of my wanting her to have her freedom and space, or if I was selfishly expecting her to call based on an epiphany that Mom and Dad may have been right about life. Regrettably, it seems my stubbornness had won out again. This is obviously counterintuitive behavior for someone who was intentionally trying to better connect. However, like clockwork, my text messages departed from my iPhone each and every morning. I could have easily pushed call; instead, I held my course. Why is it so hard for some to simply talk?

As a father, the more pressing concern was tied to her overall well-being. The fact that she was now settled in a safe place with good people was more important than extra phone calls. I was thankful for that knowledge. Yet still, I could not fully forgive myself for not doing more to reach out. Over the past ten months, I have commented about embracing change, leading, being proactive and accountable; however, sadly, I turned inward and sat idly by, waiting for the phone to ring. My focus went to what it always does—work. Some habits are extremely hard to break.

Channeling my energies, I worked to build upon my knowledge on which I was trying to impart. Wisdom. I found myself doing research, reading articles and books on the subject of wisdom and its place within our existence. My search for the true meaning of wisdom became more elusive than my ability to redirect my old habits tied to work.

In contrast to wisdom, the events of the day seemed to lack any semblance of common sense. While there was plenty of target-rich news or current event tidbits to text about, I chose to dig deeper into my efforts to compile a complete array of logical principals and sound expressions. Getting closer to the finish line, I wanted to ensure that I had not missed the opportunity to inscribe my thoughts and beliefs as I saw life in the moment. Staying the course was more important than stepping off into the stupidity of any particular day.

Wednesday, July 1

Good Morning, Em!

New Hampshire's state motto was adopted from a toast written by one of the state's most famous soldiers. General John Stark penned, "Live free or die: Death is not the worst of evils." The four simple words of "live free or die" are indelibly ingrained in your father's psyche and skin. To me, they represent the truest expression of American individualization, patriotism, and freedom.

Love, Dad

Thursday, July 2

Good Morning, Emily!

There is nothing more disappointing than learned helplessness. Seeing others waste the precious time of life that they were given is heartbreaking. Jim Collins, in reference to Admiral James Stockdale's influence, coined the term "Stockdale Paradox" and said, "You must maintain unwavering faith that you can and will prevail in the end, regardless of the difficulties, and at the same time, have the discipline to confront the most brutal facts of your current reality, whatever they might be."

Love, Dad

Good Morning, Sunshine!

What is your personal BHAG? Like putting a man on the moon, what is your personal Big Hairy Audacious Goal? Reach for the stars!

Love, Dad

Good Morning, Em!

Happy Independence Day!

On this day, our Founding Fathers, specifically Thomas Jefferson, put forth our Declaration of Independence, which in part expressed the following entitlements: "We hold these truths to be self-evident, that all men are created equal, that they are endowed by their Creator with certain unalienable Rights, that among these are Life, Liberty and the pursuit of Happiness." Thomas Jefferson was wise in offering that we had the right to pursue happiness. He understood that there was no guarantee that happiness would be bestowed upon us. We will spend the majority of our life's journey pursuing this emotional state. While this may seem worrisome, please take solace as it's a simple state of mind. Have a great day!

Love, Dad

Good Morning, Em!

Empathy is a powerful emotional tool. Having the ability to step into another's shoes and vicariously feel what another is experiencing is invaluable. Practice this often with grace and humility.

Love, Dad

Good Morning, Emily!

Give yourself a break. We tend to be harder on ourselves than anyone else around us. Don't beat yourself up if things fail to perfectly match your mind's-eye vision of the future.

Love, Dad

Good Morning, Em!

Being out of your integrity will often invite a visit from the servant of humility.

Love, Dad

Wednesday, July 8

Good Morning, Emily!

Yielding to hopelessness and a scarcity mindset will only pull you deeper into the quagmire of cynicism and self-imposed despair.

"Begin at once to live, and count each separate day as a separate life."

—Seneca

Love, Dad

Thursday, July 9

Good Morning, Sunshine!

"Everything can be taken from a man but one thing: the last of the human freedoms—to choose one's attitude in any given set of circumstances, to choose one's own way."

—Viktor Frankl

Love, Dad

Friday, July 10

Good Morning, Emily!

In some extreme circumstances, it's just better to temporarily "embrace the suck." Doing so with an open mindset will allow you to successfully navigate and move through the struggle you are facing.

Love, Dad

Saturday, July 11

Good Morning, Em!

No matter how unjust it may feel, avoid the trap of deflecting responsibility or casting blame when things go wrong or turn out differently from how you may have expected. First look inward. Only through ownership and personal accountability can we enact the change we wish to see.

Love, Dad

Sunday, July 12th

Good Morning, Emily!

"The only person you are destined to become is the person you decide to be."

—Ralph Waldo Emerson

Love, Dad

Monday, July 13

Good Morning, Emily!

The measure of our life's accomplishments will not be the accumulation of wealth, assets, trinkets, or success. It will be what good we achieved in the world.

Love, Dad

Tuesday, July 14

Good Morning, Em!

MLK was a true servant leader. He practiced this skill through his actions and in his words. Our nation is a better place today than it was in 1967, as he continually and peacefully delivered a message for change, hope, and love.

"Life's most persistent and urgent question is, 'What are you doing for others?'"

—Martin Luther King, Jr.

Love, Dad

Good Morning, Em!

While achieving some version of success is a goal for most, in the end, what matters is the content of our character. Just be the best person you can be. Be able to proudly look in the mirror and know that you took every chance, put forth maximum effort, overcame personal challenges, acted with high moral standards, served others, lived well, and loved often.

Love, Dad

Good Morning, Sunshine!

Feeling sorry for ourself or our situation will never produce any meaningful results or change. What will is simply loving ourself and acknowledging that we are worthy of love.

Love, Dad

Friday, July 17

Good Morning, Emily!

No one should ever have to martyr themselves or their families in the process of expressing free speech or standing up for freedom and what they believe in. Occupants of true civil societies should be able to withstand honest debate without the need for dishonorable behavior.

Love, Dad

Saturday, July 18

Good Morning, Em!

"Folks are usually about as happy as they make their minds up to be."

—Abraham Lincoln

Love, Dad

Sunday, July 19

Good Morning, Emily!

Life is like climbing a mountain without a top. Just when we think we have hit the peak, we soon realize the beautiful vista only opens to another challenge ahead. Pause to enjoy the view, yet do not turn back as our regrets lie at the bottom.

Love, Dad

Monday, July 20

Good Morning, Emily!

We must not abdicate or relinquish our own personal purpose and creativity to others in exchange for superficial rewards.

Love, Dad

Tuesday, July 21

Good Morning, Em!

The "what's in it for me?" crowd is undermining the values and beliefs of our country. What happened to John F Kennedy's belief and challenge that all Americans should serve the public good? His words, "Ask not what your country can do for you; ask what you can do for your country," have been discarded like disposable trinkets. Lost on many is the belief of true service and the personal engagement in the well-being of others.

I hope you have a great day!

Love, Dad

Wednesday, July 22

Good Morning, Em!

I cannot help but be extremely frustrated by and embarrassed for our nation when I see the overwhelming number of people who choose to subscribe to bully tactics or participate in being the thought police in support of a "cancel culture." We are better than this.

Love, Dad

Thursday, July 23

Good Morning, Emily!

With the exception of cleaning away actual dirt, the tactic of cleansing, whether it be ethnic groups or forms of history, is a cowardly act. Selectively altering or sanitizing history does not improve the future. Now more than ever we should heed the warnings of George Santayana's words, "Those who cannot remember the past are condemned to repeat it."

Love, Dad

Friday, July 24

Good Morning, Em!

If it seems "too good to be true it," this is a safe indicator that it probably is, so do some added due diligence. I have learned this lesson a few times in my life—usually it was not associated with a very happy ending.

Love, Dad

Saturday, July 25

Good Morning, Sunshine!

"Happiness depends more upon the internal frame of a person's own mind than on the externals in the world."

—George Washington

Love, Dad

Sunday, July 26

Good Morning, Emily!

The world is an unfair place full of unlimited possibilities. Learn to openly embrace and deal with the unexpected challenges in life. In lieu of avoiding adversity or a few rocks in the road, accept these obstacles as a way to strengthen your resilience. It may feel uncomfortable, and no one says you have to have a smile on your face when you're in the thick of it, yet know that overcoming adversity will only make you stronger.

Love, Dad

Monday, July 27

Good Morning, Emily!

I'm deeply saddened by the passing of my dear cousin, Roxanne. It seems so unfair that the youngest of my generation was taken first. I am, however, comforted by the knowledge that she is now without pain and is in a much better place. May she rest in peace.

Rose Kennedy once shared; "It has been said, 'time heals all wounds.' I do not agree. The wounds remain. In time, the mind, protecting its sanity, covers them with scar tissue and the pain lessens. But it is never gone." I tend to agree with Mrs. Kennedy. Unfortunately, the chronic pain that stems from the loss of a loved one never truly subsides. We only become accustomed to its numbness, and thus it feels like it has lessened or healed. What is healing is our subconscious mind's ability to eventually weed out the unwanted memories, only to leave the caring reminders of those people of whom we loved and lost.

Love, Dad

Tuesday, July 28

Good Morning, Emily!

More than any other, the following Bible passage has brought me courage and strength during my most difficult times, especially when I was physically in peril. "Even though I walk through the valley of the shadow of death, I fear no evil, for You are with me; Your rod and Your staff, they comfort me."

—Psalm 23:4 NASB

Love, Dad

Wednesday, July 29

Good Morning, Em!

Don't ever feel sorry for yourself. Doing so will not produce any worthwhile results. By simply loving yourself with the knowledge that you're worthy will facilitate the impact that you want to make.

Love, Dad

Thursday, July 30

Good Morning, Emily!

An epiphany, or moment of clarity for some, should be a moment for pause and even celebration. This divine inspiration should not be confused with the paranoid actions of being "woke."

Love, Dad

Friday, July 31
(sent Saturday, August 1, due to a lack of Internet service)

Good Morning, Sunshine!

Growing up, you (and your brothers) were presented with more criticism than compliments. I have come to the realization that criticism is a form of managing one's behaviors versus a more desirable approach of proactive leadership.

Love, Dad

MONTH TWELVE
THE END OF A JOURNEY

FOR THE FIRST TIME in over twenty-two years, my wife and I found ourselves without children in our home. We were now bona fide empty nesters. This new beginning felt exciting and unfamiliar. We've adapted nicely, yet the house is much quieter. There is less yelling from one floor to another to get a child's attention; however, on the flip side, our dinner table debates are much more subdued. There are many cherished remembrances, which are dearly missed. This portion of our life together has gone by in a flash, yet without delay or effort, new memories will always be made.

Sending my last message was bittersweet, as wave of emotions swept over me. I was saddened by the fact that this chapter of my journey was coming to an end and simultaneously nervous about the future. I was also curious, wondering if this project was even beneficial. Did Emily gain anything from this experience? Is she any better off? Did I correctly serve her needs and enrich her life in a manner that would matter? With this portion of my journey coming to an end, I am anxious as I feel I still have more that I want to share. I am sure there are things

I have forgotten or overlooked that may be important. More relevant or unexpected guidance may be of value, and it can be passed on so long as it is genuine and welcome. Thankfully, there is no expiration date on fatherly advice or shared wisdom.

In the conclusive words of Geoffrey Chaucer, "All good things must come to end." This proverb reminds us that nothing lasts forever; all things, beings, and situations are temporary. Early on when I set my course, I elected to do this for a finite period. Yes, it started as a temporary solution to an uneasy and complex personal problem, yet it has become much more. Now, at the end of my journey, I can see the many blessings. A formed a new habit that I can build upon. An awakening that causes me to look excitedly toward the future.

Saturday, August 1

Good Morning, Sunshine!

You're receiving two messages today, as your mom and I have been camping where there's been no signal. We hope you're doing well.

Good Morning, Em!

The power of persuasion: some of us possess this skill, yet most do not. For those of whom are truly blessed with this strength, they must have their ego squarely in check and only dispense this power judiciously with grace and humility.

Love, Dad

Good Morning, Emily!

Do not wait for things to happen in your life, and don't sacrifice your happiness for someone else's dream. Own your future outcome(s) through proactive decisions and actions. Be the creator of your own dreams.

Love, Dad

Good Morning, Sunshine!

While it was virtual, it was very nice to see you last night. Good luck on your new job. Here's my message for the day.

We fall at the mercy of our own thoughts through our lack of action when we carelessly believe the problems in our life are out of our control or lie at the feet of others.

Love, Dad

Good Morning, Emily!

"Remember how long you've been putting this off, how many extensions the gods gave you, and you didn't use them. At some point you have to recognize what the world it is that you belong to; what power rules it and from what source you spring; that there is a limit to the time assigned you, and if you don't use it to free yourself it will be gone and will never return."

—Marcus Aurelius

Love, Dad

Good Morning, Em!

Using "sir" and "ma'am" when addressing people is usually associated with Southerners, but the practice is believed to have originated in eighteenth century England. Either way, it's just a sign of good manners and politeness. As a side benefit, these simple gestures help to build trust and respect.

Love, Dad

Good Morning, Emily!

No joke, laughter is the best medicine:

-It decreases stress.

-It increases immune cells.

-It increases infection-fighting antibodies.

-It can temporarily relieve pain.

-It releases feel-good chemicals (endorphins).

-It puts a smile on your face, which is addictive.

Find reasons to laugh often.

Love,

Dad

Good Morning, Em!

"It is what it is!" is not a proverb; it is an idiomatic statement. It is a casual expression used to characterize a frustrating or challenging situation. The user accepts and believes that an outcome cannot be changed and must just be accepted. Frankly, most times the user is unwilling to put forth the effort to effect change.

Love, Dad

Saturday, August 8

Good Morning, Emily!

The path to freedom must pass through a world of discipline. Without discipline, we will also lack the courage and integrity to achieve honorable results.

Love, Dad

Sunday, August 9

Good Morning, Emily!

One of the greatest gifts we can give others is our ability to serve them by expressing love, raising their spirits, and helping them feel better. In return, we are loved.

Love, Dad

Monday, August 10

Good Morning, Em!

"We shall overcome because the arc of the moral universe is long but bends toward justice."

—Martin Luther King, Jr.

Love, Dad

Tuesday, August 11

Good Morning, Emily!

We cannot change the past, yet we can most certainly change the future. We are the author of our own life's script. If we choose, we can be the hero, or we can allow a villain to creep in. One so vile that it manipulates our thoughts and way of being. Be the hero of your own story. Know that you can proactively change anything that does not fit your vision for the future. Be your own hero.

Love, Dad

Wednesday, August 12

Good Morning, Emily!

Ego vs. Empathy: One end of the spectrum only thinks of oneself, whereas the opposite pole focuses on others. At times, a healthy ego can be effective if kept in check, yet more can be accomplished when we lead with our heart.

Love, Dad

Thursday, August 13

Good Morning, Sunshine!

"All things are created twice," says Stephen R. Covey. "There's a mental or first creation, and a physical or second creation to all things." This means we have twice the ability to create a better future for ourselves. Or, we have the ability to improve our physical creation even when we have a negative mental creation in our own mind's eye.

Love, Dad

Friday, August 14

Good Morning, Emily!

Don't feel pressured in always needing or having an answer. Honestly saying, "I don't know!" can be a humbling experience, yet having a creative and thoughtful question is empowering.

Love, Dad

Saturday, August 15

Good Morning, Sunshine!

"No one can persuade another to change. Each of us guards a gate of change that can only be opened from the inside. We cannot open the gate of another, either by argument or emotional appeal."

—Marilyn Ferguson

In addition to personal choice (voluntarily opening the gate), input and ownership are required elements needed to achieve change within a team.

Love, Dad

Sunday, August 16

Good Morning, Emily!

Be kind to people; treat people as you would like to be treated. Embrace the Golden Rule of "Do unto others as you would have them do unto you," as stated in Luke 6:31 (NIV). Similarly, to earn respect, one must first unconditionally show and give respect.

Love, Dad

Monday, August 17

Good Morning, Emily!

"Pride is an awesome force as long as it is balanced between humility and confidence. If you let it creep too far in either direction, it will become destructive."

—Jocko Willink

Love, Dad

Tuesday, August 18

Good Morning, Em!

Agreeing for the sake of being agreeable and/or walking on eggshells around others only undermines our own integrity. Be yourself; openly and constructively speak your mind as appropriate.

Love, Dad

Wednesday, August 19

Good Morning, Emily!

It's important to understand one's weaknesses, yet it's paramount to focus your energies on enhancing your strengths.

Love, Dad

Thursday, August 20

Good Morning, Em!

Seeking or demanding instant gratification of life's pleasures will only lead to a narcissistic lifestyle.

Love, Dad

Friday, August 21

Good Morning, Sunshine!

"May we think of freedom, not as the right to do as we please, but as the opportunity to do what is right."

—Rev. Peter Marshall

Love, Dad

Saturday, August 22

Good Morning, Sunshine!

You are the David in the Goliath of your life. With time, you will build the skills necessary to overcome this immense challenge. Have faith in your ability to win over this imposing figure.

Love, Dad

Good Morning, Em!

Stephen R. Covey' second habit reminds us to "Begin with the End in Mind." Build the habit of visualizing the end result of what you are seeking. By doing so, you find the pathway to success much easier.

Love, Dad

Good Morning, Em!

I'm deeply saddened by the overwhelming number of people who choose an irreversible final solution for their life when so many others would give everything for just one more day in the glory of this world.

Love, Dad

P.S. We all matter, and our lives have purpose. Thus, behind love, hope is an incredibly beautiful feeling and desire.

Good Morning, Emily!

Vilfredo Pareto is credited with "The Pareto Principle," which states, "Eighty percent of your results come from only 20 percent of your efforts." This does not mean that we only apply maximum effort 20 percent of the time. However, it does reinforce the fact that a small portion of meaningful activity can produce great results.

Love, Dad

Good Morning, Sunshine!

The wisdom of youth has not exponentially increased at the same rate of growth as technology and the availability of information. Frankly, it seems just the opposite has occurred. It appears as if the effects of the Digital Age have temporarily stunted the development of street smarts and/or common sense in many children and some of their parents. We shouldn't be convinced that all of life's knowledge is simply held in our hands.

Love, Dad

Thursday, August 27

Good Morning, Em!

As children and young adults, we learn what we live. As parents, we cannot easily teach our children to be hungry (gritty). Similar to wisdom, the trait of grit is hard-earned. The resolve and courage needed to overcome adversity will be revealed over time from life's teachings. Look for and cherish these pivotal moments. While some may test you, or even try to tear you down, know there is a valuable lesson in each event.

Love, Dad

Friday, August 28

Good Morning, Em!

It is key that we seek reason and objective truth before setting off on a quest in search for an alternative history. I believe Condoleezza Rice summed it up correctly: "When you start wiping out your history, sanitizing your history to make you feel better, it's a bad thing,"

Love, Dad

Good Morning, Emily!

Luck or good fortune? I believe we possess the means to create our own luck, good or bad. Through our actions, we hold in our hands the ability to live a blessed life.

Love, Dad

Good Morning, Em!

The truth is the truth. No different than fiction versus facts or the difference between darkness and light, there cannot be a version of darkness that equals light. I am hopeful that one day, society will demand only to see the light.

Love, Dad

Good Morning, Em!

Getting hung up on "who we are" or "what we do" professionally can distract us from our true calling in life. Martha Grimes reminds us that "we don't know who we are until we see what we can do." Therefore, go forward with full confidence in yourself and find your "do."

Love, Dad

Tuesday, September 1

Good Morning, Em!

Stress is an emotional state, and we all experience it from time to time. The key to overcoming its gravitational pull is to recognize the early warning signs and proactively manage them. In short bursts, stress can help to motivate, yet in a chronic state, if allowed, it can tie your feet to the ground. Recalling the key tenets of the Serenity Prayer has helped me to break free from its grips.

Love, Dad

Wednesday, September 2

Good Morning, Emily!

Eventually we all find our way in life. It is incumbent upon our internal fortitude and personal courage to continually push ourselves beyond our current station or self-imposed limitations. In the immortal words of Winston Churchill, "Success is not final; failure is not fatal: It is the courage to continue that counts." Know that the struggles and pain we feel in life as well as the glory and love we experience is the tempering that forges us into who we become as individuals. Trust in these shaping cycles, and never allow your courage to fade.

Love, Dad

Good Morning, Sunshine!

"There are people, who the more you do for them, the less they will do for themselves."

—Jane Austen

Equally as true, we are unable to lead others if we are unwilling to lead ourselves first.

Love, Dad

Friday, September 4

Good Morning, Em!

Each day we make hundreds if not thousands of decisions. Most are trivial, like choosing what clothes to wear, whether or not to make the bed, or deciding on breakfast. There are also monumental decisions that we make, such as deciding if (or who) we will marry, what career path we pursue, or where we choose to live. Then there are the foundational decisions. These are our choices regarding which principles or values we will follow throughout the course of our life. Will we live a life of integrity, choose to serve others, or select a more selfish pathway? Do we see the abundance in life or choose to live a life of scarcity? While most of the trivial and monumental decisions can easily be reversed. Our foundational decisions greatly affect our paradigm of life. These tendencies will ultimately color how we make other choices. Our foundational decisions cannot simply be unraveled as they go to the core of who we choose to be and fundamentally are the root of who we become.

Love, Dad

Good Morning, Em!

As humans, we come equipped with the greatest strength known within the animal kingdom. It is clearly not our vision, hearing, or sense of smell. Neither is it our cherished opposable thumbs. However, it is our conscious ability to pause between stimulus and response, and it is our corresponding free will to choose how we respond. Victor E. Frankl correctly observed this when he said, "Between stimulus and response there is a space. In that space is our power to choose our response. In our response lies our growth and our freedom."

Love, Dad

Good Morning, Emily!

In the words of Stephen R. Covey, "The first choice we make each and every day is, 'Will we act upon life, or will we merely be acted upon?'" The power of positive thoughts and concrete actions will lead to worthy results.

Love, Dad

Monday, September 7

Good Morning, Emily!

Happy Labor Day!

This is the last daily text message. You might be wondering why I picked today. Labor Day is a holiday set aside to honor the social and economic achievements and contributions of American workers. It is the hard work and spirit of these workers that has forged the strength, well-being, and prosperity of this great nation. In keeping with this observance, it seemed only fitting that I wrap up this series on Labor Day. Not because this has been an effort for me, but more importantly, the culmination of messages composed and sent constituted a pure labor of love.

Over the past year I have shared my personal feelings, thoughts, beliefs, opinions, and pithy quotes as well as many thought-provoking quotations from numerous thought leaders. And yes, maybe a couple of lecturing comments from Dad were thrown in as well. Nonetheless, I hope this effort has lifted your spirit, put a smile on your face, and illustrated the genuine love that a father has for his daughter. You are a strong, smart, and beautiful woman who can do whatever you put your effort and heart into. Go forth and Do Better!

Love, Dad

PART TWO

Wisdom of the Common Man

DO BETTER!

THE HARDEST THING FOR any parent is to see their child hurting, struggling, or—god forbid—anything worse. Naturally, when our children are little, we want to reach down and pick them up or hug them when these events occur. When they are adults, the solution is not always as easy.

One of my reasons for embarking on this journey was the fact that I did not fully understand or could not appreciate what it was like to be a young woman. Now in her early twenties, I could see that my daughter was struggling. Unsure of the root cause for her anguish, I wanted to help. It would not take a rocket scientist to point out that more than a hug was required.

I would submit that while I had hoped this endeavor has helped us come closer, I am not sure if it helped me see the world any differently through her eyes. I hope I have! I hope I did not rush to judgement and I have opened my eyes to understand that while she is my daughter, she did not have the same upbringing as I. Her life experiences, daily challenges, external motivators, and environmental conditions would understandably cause her to see the world through a different contextual lens. Therefore, while I can have empathy for her, I cannot genuinely appreciate what it is like to be in her shoes. While not vastly insightful, this revelation does not free me from the responsibility to Do Better!

Looking back, the original hypothesis behind my unscientific theory and course of action could have been the following; "The delivery of thoughtful insights, guidance, and goodwill (wisdom) through the means of structured and consistent messaging will reinforce the attributes of positive self-confidence within the recipient as well as strengthen the bonds of a father-daughter relationship."

In support of this theory, I became curious and found myself looking for evidence to see if text messaging would provide the desired stimulus or motivation. I wanted to know if this intervention of sorts was going to be effective. Did I stumble onto a new and legitimate means of supporting my daughter? A quick search discovered that "text messaging interventions" and the use of texting for aiding others was not a novel idea. Less than five minutes of digging on the Internet revealed that studies and scholarly papers have been in existence for over a decade. Short Message Service (SMS), or text messages, have been used to promote heathy behaviors in adults; from battling substance abuse, promoting physical activity and weight loss, to the self-management of diabetes. I was a fool for thinking that I might have devised a new method of electronic therapy. I should have known better; businesses have been using this technology as a customer solution for years. In the sage words of William Shakespeare, "The fool doth think he is wise, but the wise man knows himself to be a fool." In this case, I feel a little foolish.

As much as many would like to believe, conventional wisdom, common sense, and street smarts are not automatically passed down in our DNA. I was recently reminded of this by an unimpeachable quote highlighted within a take-out fortune cookie: "We don't receive wisdom; we must discover it for ourselves after a journey that no one can take for us or spare us." This poses the question: Have my efforts over the past year been in vain? In retrospect, it also bares the following questions: As it relates to personal wisdom, are the culmination of these specifically expressed thoughts only unique to me? Will this collection of words only truly resonate with me, or will they fall short in the form of sentimental hogwash? Will they have their desired effect on the recipient?

Like me, you are probably also wondering, "Did this work? Did twelve months of daily text messages improve your relationship with your daughter?" I was eager to know, and I was hopeful that my efforts created a real impact on Emily other than simply crowding out data capacity on her cell phone. There was only one way to find out, and I merely needed to ask. Armed with good intentions, in early August I emailed Emily the following message in hopes of triggering further dialog.

August 9, 2020

Dear Emily,

I am writing, as I would genuinely appreciate your feedback. Over the past year I have been sending daily messages because I believed they would be of value to you. I have come to realize more now than ever that I embarked on a journey without recognizing where the end destination should be. Or, more importantly, if you even wanted to go along for the ride. As your father, I want to be supportive of you, as most parents should. I truly want to understand your perspective and how you see the world. To do this, I have initiated further dialogue with a few questions below. If you have other insights that you wish to share (even if you feel that they may be difficult), I want to hear them. I do want to understand.

I look forward to hearing from you.

Love, Dad

Question No. 1: How did the offered insight (daily messages) show up for you?

Question No. 2: What were the "Top 3" insights that resonated with you the most, and why?

Question No. 3: What was the greatest takeaway (or impact) for you that resulted from this experience?

Five weeks later, I followed up with a brief second message reinforcing my appreciation for any feedback she wished to offer. With no response in return, I elected to leave things alone, allowing her more time to collect her thoughts. However, in the back of my mind, doubts began to shadow my hopes that she would eventually convey her feelings. To my surprise, my questions would be answered.

On the last evening of the month (September 30), in a conversation with my daughter, I realized that she left home with more baggage than I could have possibly imagined. The feedback that I so desperately sought was now coming home to

198 Norman W. Holden

roost. Regrettably, a message that I wrote earlier in the year (on February 9) was received in a much different context than it was written. She rebuked this message as a frontal attack, claiming that I had told her "she was ruining our family."

Shocked, saddened, and frustrated, I began to question her response as well as my own motives and actions. So, what really just occurred? Was this a victim mindset looking for blame to be placed for the sadness she was feeling, or was I being an insensitive, overbearing father without a clue? As always, the truth lies somewhere in the middle. Soon after our phone call, I realized the answers that I was hoping for and expecting were not going to be delivered. As requested, Emily did provide feedback; it was crystal clear that her scars from the past year were still fresh and had not yet healed. While she did not say it directly, I sensed that she was struggling, and our relationship felt estranged.

Frankly, I was naive to expect a different result. While my inner eye saw growth and improvement, the reality for Emily was much different. Feeling the remnants of pain derived several months earlier, she was still reeling from her version of the message. An email that outlined the pain my wife and I were experiencing was interpreted as a declaration of a more heinous offense. In my view, this could not be further from the truth. Were we struggling? Yes! However, as her parents, we wanted nothing but the best for her. Attempting to guide her as best we knew how, we wanted her to grow to be the truest version of herself that she could be. Nothing more and nothing less.

In hindsight, I could have and should have been a better father and leader. My initial reaction was of frustration that we were on polar opposite ends of the spectrum. It is obvious that much more time is needed to heal these wounds. My efforts to bridge the gap between us may have put a few small stones in place, yet it really did not build the structure that we both required. Confronted with this revelation, I will not give up, nor am I deterred. I will admit my dismay, as I wanted so much for this to be the instrument that brought us closer. Maybe someday it will. At the present, it is an open sore.

While I certainly do not feel my efforts were in vain, I can see that I have much more work to do to achieve the desired results. Obviously, one year of text messages does not equate or offset ten years of neglect. My neglect, even though unintentional, was the result of not having these conversations sooner during her formative years. The void that I created allowed others outside of our home with much stronger voices than mine to creep in. Frankly, I now recognize that these unwanted voices had poisoned her beliefs, opinions, and values. Many things that I do not agree with. Unfortunately, these shaped and solidified the beliefs that she now stands on.

I hope that someday we are able to make inroads and clear the air. I very much want to have an open relationship with my daughter. One that allows us to openly communicate, where we can speak our minds with an open heart and without the other side feeling cornered. The publication of this book may only exacerbate things or delay our progress even more. As an outsider looking in, I hope the reader sees that this father genuinely wants the best for his children. The truth is, I want Emily to find happiness, fulfillment, and success.

Prior to starting my messaging routine, I feel I made attempts to "seek first to understand" (Covey, 1989). I now feel in some ways I have still missed the mark. My early prescription of what I feel she should be doing or feeling is based on my perspective of the world and not through her lenses or paradigm. In lieu of truly seeking to understand her needs, I began down a path with what I thought she needed or wanted. In my haste and partial understanding, most likely I wrongly diagnosed what issues deeply concerned her. My actions had a lesser effect, as I am now sure that my words came across as advising and not encouraging.

Ultimately, it was my intent to send her simple words of encouragement. Maybe they came through on a micro level. Meaning, a message here or there on a given day may have pierced through, rung true, and improved her outlook for the day. On a macro level, my efforts may have fallen flat, failing to have the full affect. At the time of writing this, I have come to realize that my twenty-three-year-old daughter does not currently embrace my beliefs, maybe the thirty-three or forty-three-year-old Emily will someday see the value. I am hopefully optimistic that we will both experience long-term benefits from this endeavor. Only time will tell.

Even though things have not progressed as I had wanted, the past year has been a greater labor of love for me than I could have ever hoped for. The hours spent deliberating on numerous topics, looking up the meanings of words, phrases, and quotations proved extremely therapeutic for me. This journey has caused me to reflect upon my beliefs and way of being more than any personal assessment or leadership course could have promised. This process has fully awakened the right side of my brain. The intuitive, creative, and imaginative side. More than she will ever imagine, I am internally grateful for the opportunity that Emily has given to me to express my innermost thoughts. I am truly thankful to her.

Many times throughout the yearlong journey, I asked myself, "Should I continue?" When I felt my messages falling on possible deaf ears, I often experienced a shame response, telling myself that I must have failed her in some way because I didn't get the warm responses of love and gratitude I was seeking. I wasn't being told all the ways I was being supportive or loving or wise. Maybe I was not as good a parent as I thought ... But wait! Parenthood isn't about me! It's about giving and sacrifice and ... if I'm honest ... a lot of humility. I was going into this hoping to get a result instead of offering what I could and waiting for the crop to reach full harvest, which takes time. I expected my harvest to bear fruit in my personal one-year timeline, but young adults have to go through their own battles, trials, and bruises to come full circle years down the path in order to really understand who we are to them, why we do what we do, and that it's okay if we were not perfect. Suddenly, the self-pity question of "Should I continue?" answered itself. "Yes!" I heard myself say aloud. "I will always continue to connect, be the first to reach out, offer love and acceptance, and have faith that the timing of Emily's wisdom is her path." I felt at peace, finally understanding that what I hoped was her yearlong journey was really mine, which I then shared with her. My continued growth will only increase my openness and availability and patience as she traverses through life. Patience was finally replaced for the timeline I had placed on our relationship. And I can now let my unsettled mind find peace with our past and live into a better future.

This experience has made me realize that as parents, we can always question our results. "What could we have done better or differently?" I was recently reminded that you cannot raise your kids twice. Frankly, we do the best job that we can with the knowledge and tools that we have. Personally, a decade ago I would have struggled to generate the same level of insights that I produced over the past year. Honestly, I did not have the patience or self-discipline to pause long enough from work to look beyond my day-to-day existence. With that said, given the opportunity to do things again, I would work to improve all of my personal relationships in an effort to facilitate real and meaningful conversations.

In my opinion, earned wisdom is the connection of experiential dots throughout one's life. No two people will have the same pattern because we are all genetically different at birth (apart from identical twins). These differences are further expanded based upon our unique life experiences, values, and beliefs. The culmination of these differences would cause each us to see life's wisdom through our own individualized contextual lens. This conclusion leads me to believe that only a small portion of my shared thoughts, messages, or affirmations will hit their desired mark or move the needle. Consequently, they will not mean the same to my daughter (the recipient) as they do for me. As her life progresses and she grows older, the percentage of this shared wisdom may ring truer, yet there is no guarantee, even though we share roughly fifty percent of the same genetic code.

Like my children, I have continued to learn and grow. My paradigm is much different (and better) now then it was when I stumbled through my daughter's adolescent years. In the end, I hesitate to say that this journey required a high level of technical expertise on my part. Simply, it required me to grow up and realize that we are conditioned to see the world through the making of our own contextual lenses. My view of the world is and will always be different than my daughter's, but that is okay.

Even though this unique approach did not reverse a decade of missed conversations, it did reinforce some simple yet concrete conclusions. First things first, speed kills. Dad's intuition and wisdom is no match for the artificial intelligence that is baked into today's social medial. Face it, Instagram, Facebook, Twitter, or any other platforms' algorithms are operating at warp speed as compared to our own grey matter. Parents do not stand a chance in a foot race with technology. Secondly, positive intermittent reinforcement should come from Mom and Dad, not social media. If you want to interrupt or break the spell, consistently express and show your love through action. Be firm and demanding, yet incredibly supportive.

Lastly, do not wait or make excuses. Put down your devices and talk. As a parent, the best thing we can do for our children is to limit device and social media usage. There is a reason why the inventors of this technology do not allow their own children to use it or enforce limited exposure to these platforms. Replace screen time with face-to-face time. There is no better substitute. Talk, have a meaningful conversation, and most importantly— listen.

While I inferred earlier that we tend to do the best we can with the tools we have at the time, I put forth the challenge for all of us to Do Better! If we choose, we all have the ability to improve the world around us. Helen Keller said, "Character cannot be developed in ease and quiet. Only through experience of trial and suffering can the soul be strengthened, ambition inspired, and success achieved." We all struggle in life, most not as much as Hellen Keller, yet any meaningful journey is worth the struggle.

WISDOM'S PAST

IN MY OPINION, WISDOM has been around since the dawn on human civilization. Early wisdom had to have occurred as soon as we mastered our conscious ability to make levelheaded decisions and choose our course of action between stimulus and response.

It is probably safe to conclude that the earliest forms of wisdom came about in our efforts not to be eaten by a much larger and scarier saber-toothed foe. Call it instinct or the mastery of knowledge and hard-earned experience, but either way, we can safely assume that the wisest among us managed to dodge being a tasty appetizer.

Wisdom is defined by Merriam-Webster as:

- "knowledge that is gained by having many experiences in life,

- "the natural ability to understand things that most other people cannot understand, and

- "knowledge of what is proper or reasonable: good sense or judgment"

There is a distinct difference between wisdom and knowledge. Knowledge is simply knowing, and it alone does not equate to wisdom. Neither does experience alone. The primary difference between the act of knowing and being wise is that wisdom requires heathy portions of knowledge, experience, perspective, and the capacity for sound judgment. Again, it is easy to surmise that early humans evolved by using these assets combined with sound judgement to avoid becoming prehistoric scat.

Fast forward a few million years, and wisdom is formalized in Scripture. Over the ages, humans have sought to understand the meanings of life. While religion in one form or another has provided this primary pathway, I firmly believe wisdom is one of the few conduits to those desired insights. Personally, I am not a subscriber to a specific religious denomination or formalized religion in general. I was baptized Christian and married into the Catholic Church, yet other than attending Mass with my wife and children for special occasions, I have not followed the strict teachings of the Christian church. I am somewhat of a mutt when it comes to religion and faith. I have faith in a higher power and a firm personal spirituality. I also feel that the majority of religious beliefs are grounded with good intentions and are based on the act of love (serving others).

Why am I sharing this personal perspective? Simply, I wanted to expose my beliefs for what they are without the "holier than thou" pretense. I have zero religious authority, yet when it comes to the teachings of wisdom, one cannot ignore the religious roots of this principle. At a minimum, the reference to wisdom appears over two hundred times in the King James Version.

Within the Bible, wisdom is represented by Solomon, who is best displayed in Proverbs. For those readers who are unfamiliar with Solomon, he was the king of kings, the son of David, and the king of Israel. In plain speak, Solomon was a particularly good and wise man, and Proverbs contains truths and words of wisdom from his lessons in life. In addition to the proverbs of Solomon, there is one set of passages that illustrates why Solomon was placed on the mantle of wisdom. In 2 Chronicles, Solomon demonstrates his desire to practice the principles of wisdom. In a desire to better serve his people, Solomon asked God for the gift of wisdom above riches, fame, or health.

2 Chronicles 1:10 KJV

"Give me now wisdom and knowledge, that I may go out and come in before this people: for who can judge this thy people, that is so great?"

2 Chronicles 1:11 KJV

"And God said to Solomon, Because this was in thine heart, and thou hast not asked riches, wealth, or honour, nor the life of thine enemies, neither yet hast asked long life; but hast asked wisdom and knowledge for thyself, that thou mayest judge my people, over whom I have made thee king:"

2 Chronicles 1:12 KJV

"Wisdom and knowledge is granted unto thee; and I will give thee riches, and wealth, and honour, such as none of the kings have had that have been before thee, neither shall there any after thee have the like."

Within these scriptures, the reader can easily surmise that Solomon understood the need for servant leadership and the potential of divine wisdom.

In Proverbs as well as other parts of the Bible, wisdom is personified as a woman. It makes sense that the wise elder in the tribe was associated with the older women. In ancient times, older women were revered for their wisdom because they tended to be the keeper of primal mysteries and tribal genealogy. This belief is further reinforced when reflecting upon the fact that women historically are the teachers, caregivers, and life providers of the family unit. Whereas the men tended to play a stark opposite role as warriors, hunters, and gatherers. Frankly, it makes perfect sense. A woman's intuition is better honed than a man's. And what man would want to feel the wrath of a scorned woman? Suffice to say, Solomon was nobody's fool.

Fast forward a few hundred more years, and wisdom is redefined by modern man. The Old English etymology (OED, 2020) of the word wisdom is "knowledge, learning, experience" and stems from *wis*, which means "learned, sagacious, cunning; sane; prudent, discreet; experienced; having the power of discerning and judging rightly," plus *dom*, which refers to "domain (kingdom), collection of persons (officialdom), rank or station (earldom), or general condition (freedom)." When combined, these roots translate to "a domain (kingdom) of experience." (This reaffirms the importance King Solomon's wisdom.)

While wisdom is rooted in religion and most books on the subject are of religious nature, it can be found in many other written forms. Many of the leadership, personal, and professional development books available on the shelves are another primary delivery method for sharing different themes of wisdom. Take, for example, the late Stephen R. Covey's book *The 7 Habits of Highly Effective People.* This self-help guide contains more thought-provoking wisdom than most religious equals. Over the ages, there have been many great thought leaders, from Aristotle to Thomas Jefferson to Viktor E. Frankl and, more recently, Jim Collins and Patrick Lencioni, just to name a few. Each presented based on their unique circumstances, yet all have provided their pearls of wisdom as they see it. As the reader, we identify with those pearls that resonate with our contextual beliefs. Indelibly, the proverbs of Solomon have stood the test of time, as wisdom is universal and timeless. It does not require repackaging or a New Age spin.

We all have insights to share, and there are reems of books on leadership and personal development. Combined with millions of webpages of information, there is more documented knowledge available at our fingertips than we could consume in a lifetime. Frankly, there is too much, yet there are some real gems in all that noise.

Wisdom is not just for religious people or the so-called elites. All of us have the ability to seek it out and use her teachings. Wisdom, while it can be profound, discoverable, and even divine, is only deeply appreciated by the experiencer (initial creator). As most of us know, wisdom is earned through a life of lessons learned, some joyous occasions, and many hard knocks. In the end, it really comes down to what actions we put into place as a result of these personalized experiences, gained knowledge, and acquired wisdom.

A FATHER'S REFLECTION ON WISDOM

As PREVIOUSLY STATED, I am not an expert on the subject of wisdom or the associated principles that have stood the test of time. I am an expert on the wisdom that I have accumulated over the course of five-plus decades. Much of which has come into clarity over the later years of my life. Gained over time, this knowledge has been at my fingertips, put into play as needed, yet the contextual lenses of my being did not fully align until more recently.

This experience has taught me that earned wisdom is the connection of experiential dots amassed throughout one's life. With the caveat that most principles of wisdom are universal and true, no two people's patterns are inherently the same. Our earned wisdom is as uniquely different as our fingerprints, and our life's paradigm is also individualized. Ultimately, wisdom lives within an infinite mindset. It is not gained or achieved through the "I want it now!" philosophy that so many have come to expect. It cannot be ordered through Amazon Prime nor can it be dispensed via an expedient take-out service. It is hard earned through real-life experiences that can only develop over time. Even then, not all of us pause long enough to embrace the knowledge gained. On the bright side, once earned, wisdom can never be taken away. It is yours for eternity, it is just up to you and what you choose to do with it.

While I am confident about wisdom's origins, I am not sure if at the end of this journey I am any closer to understanding the inner workings of a women's mind. I hope my efforts as a father to do better are beneficial and have made a difference in my daughter's life. Hopefully, my words and aphorisms have provided some value for her (and you), and I have not simply filled the void of silence.

Frankly, this endeavor has left me with more questions than answers; thus is the power of wisdom. Not all her teachings are easily consumed; many require hours, days, and even years to understand or appreciate their full enlightenment. I am left wondering, *Has this endeavor moved the needle? Did I connect intrinsically, or did I simply produce a memoir of my own personal beliefs and create an heirloom for my children's children?* Only time will tell.

Blessed with the strengths of "Context" and "Strategic," found in an enlightening book called *Strengths Finder*, I tend to look back in my personal history because that is where the answers lie for me. An ability that has served me well, I look back to understand the present. While not absolute, the best predictor of the future can be from the past. Able to easily spot the relevant patterns and issues, I can translate this information, discard the irrelevant data, and create a stainable vision for the future. Hopefully, history will tell me that my efforts have borne fruit. As a father (and leader) I cannot wait. I must act and create a better future.

Throughout my career, I have had the benefit of taking many personal assessments, as well as being engaged in hours of leadership training and professional coaching. This combined with reading hundreds of articles and books on leadership, self-improvement, business, and personal development, I feel I have a solid foundation of knowledge and life experiences to tap into. Based on these teachings, I have formed the opinion that wisdom comes in many forms, like the thousand flickering lights of faraway stars. When wisdom appears before us, we have a choice. We can take these miracles for granted, assuming they will just reappear the very next evening for our viewing pleasure. Or we can stop, gaze, wonder, and reflect on what we just witnessed and from this experience, translate this knowledge into sound judgement. I am a firm believer that through internalization and retrospection, we can draw the full value from one's wisdom and analyze the truths as we travel through life.

Alone, looking back at one's life and deciphering its most potent teachings is a powerful experience. On a grander scale, the process of reflecting upon and accumulating sage advice or words of wisdom from said experiences is another entire challenge within its own right. Some could argue that these efforts and this book constitutes a simple list of principles, desired behaviors, and my personal beliefs and commentary on current affairs. Producing daily content was more than a personal validation. It has awoken change that I could not have foreseen. In the simplest terms, the profound words of Mario Quintana sum up my transformation, "Books don't change the world, people change the world, books only change people."

I am also certain that our life's attainment of wisdom is the culmination of invisible threads that are woven together over time. We are inherently tied together, generation after generation, through the people we meet, our travels, experiences, and relationships. These threads are further strengthened by our actions and from the actions of others, gained knowledge, and the mastery of our own contentment. At the core of life's tapestry is the strongest and unlimited fiber of love. The act of loving and serving others is only further enhanced by the sharing of divine wisdom.

Lastly, I cannot in good faith end this chapter without offering the following confessional. While I believe in the words that I have expressed within, I will humbly say that in my past I have not always honored these beliefs or lived up to the full integrity of these words and their meanings. No different than anyone else, from time to time I have had my fair share of struggles. On occasions, I have tripped and fallen, yet I have always done my utmost to get back up and continue to move forward in a positive direction. As I get older, remaining in integrity with myself becomes easier and more prominent. I cannot change my past, yet I have the absolute power to control my future attitude and actions. Though I have not always walked the straightest line, there is a deep determination within me that wants to Do Better!

AFTERWORD

THIS BOOK WOULD NOT be complete without sharing where the inspiration of the title Do Better! came from. These were the parting words from my youngest cousin (Roxanne Smith) after a family vacation in Bridgton, Maine. In lieu of the typical "Goodbye!" "Take Care!" or "Safe Travels!" my fun-loving cousin Rox exclaimed "Do Better!" Her response caught me by surprise, and it brought a big smile to my face. I repeated back, "Do Better?" She replied, "Yeah, why just say goodbye when you can establish higher expectations for the future." Her farewell directive stuck. Thanks to the uncanny advice of my dear cousin, Rox's "Do Better!" salutation altered my attitude and corresponding actions toward an internal dilemma. For this, I will always be grateful.

What was originally a six-month prognosis, Roxanne was able to battle the cancer demon for more than three years. Sadly, she passed on July 25, 2020, one week shy of a year from when I last saw her in person and was able to give her a hug goodbye. The freest spirit of the group, Roxanne was the youngest and the opposite bookend from me of our generation. Her untimely departure from our lives only reinforces the importance that we must take the opportunity we have been given to make the most of each and every day.

Roxanne will be greatly missed, and she will always have a place in my heart.

Roxanne and me in Maine: August 3, 2019

EPILOUGE

In early December 2020, I received an unexpected response from Emily regarding my earlier inquires and request for her feedback. Emily's email was a welcomed surprise that brought forth an immediate warmth to my heart. As a father, I could not be happier to have received her message. At a time when I needed it the most, her words were a much-needed tug at the fiber of love within my being. In an instant, the weight of doubt and struggle was lifted.

> Dad,
>
> I'm sorry this took so long for me to respond. I guess I've been pretty caught up in work this past month. I hope everything's been going well for you and that December is off to a good start. I have taken some time to reflect on the questions you sent me, and hope that my answers provide the information you are looking for.
>
> *Looking back, were there any positive benefits from me sending you daily messages?*

After thinking back on the daily messages, the biggest benefit seemed to be that we were communicating, even briefly, at least once a day. I also appreciated the fact that I was able to learn more about your thoughts and views of the world. I believe that everyone has beneficial thoughts and experiences that the people around them can learn about to grow personally."

Also, were there one or two messages that truly resonated with you?

Wednesday, September 18

While continuous improvement is a noble effort, chasing perfection is a fool's errand. Push yourself to improve and become more skilled where your passions take you.

Saturday, September 28

Be true to yourself. Be authentic and be real.

Wednesday, November 6

Be committed to something bigger than yourself.

Again, I'm sorry that it took me so long to respond to this email. I hope my answers help you out.

Love,

Emily

ABOUT THE AUTHOR

NORMAN W. HOLDEN was born and raised in the "Granite State" of New Hampshire. This first-time author artfully taps into his own ground-up evolution and life experiences. Methodically consolidating over thirty-five years in various leadership roles within the concrete construction industry, he is able to provide thoughtful insights from a common man's perspective. His down-to-earth retelling of his personal journey of wisdom is a refreshing approach to centuries-old beliefs. A proud father of three, Norman and his wife live outside of Denver in the front range of the Rocky Mountains.

QUOTATION INDEX

REFERENCES

Covey, Stephen R. (1989). *The 7 Habits of Highly Effective People*, Fraklin Covey.

JMW. (2019). "Being a Leader and the Effective Exercise of Leadership," New York.

KJV. (2020, June). Retrieved from King James Bible Online: https://www.kingjamesbibleonline.org/

M-W. (2020, June). Retrieved from Merriam-Webster: https://www.merriam-webster.com/

OED. (2020, June). Retrieved from Online Etymology Dictionary: https://www.etymonline.com/

Rath, Tom (2007). *Strengths Finder 2.0*. New York, NY: The Gallup Organization.